D1376098

step into the
STORY

B 144 01

Resource Room
Church House
9 The Close
WINCHESTER
SO23 9LS
Tel: 01962 624760

Text copyright © Margaret Spivey and Anna Jean 2003
Illustrations copyright © Jane Taylor 2003
The authors assert the moral right
to be identified as the authors of this work

Published by
The Bible Reading Fellowship
First Floor, Elsfield Hall
15–17 Elsfield Way, Oxford OX2 8FG
ISBN 1 84101 002 2

First published 2003
10 9 8 7 6 5 4 3 2 1 0
All rights reserved

Acknowledgments
Unless otherwise stated, scripture quotations are taken from the Good News Bible
published by The Bible Societies/HarperCollins Publishers Ltd, UK © American Bible
Society 1966, 1971, 1976, 1992, used with permission.

Scripture quotations from the *Contemporary English Version* © American Bible Society
1991, 1992, 1995. Used by permission/Anglicizations © British and Foreign Bible
Society 1997.

A catalogue record for this book is available from the British Library

Printed and bound in Malta

step into the
STORY

20 story and activity sessions for creative learning

Margaret Spivey and Anna Jean

'Step into the Roots of Christianity' is dedicated to
Carolyn Waite and her co-workers at Christ Church, Clevedon.
(Margaret Spivey)

'Step into the Stories of Jesus' is dedicated to
my three amazing children, Becki, Bethany and Alec,
and my equally amazing mum, Grace.

And to Stuart Graham—who provided me with much-needed fresh inspiration
when I was running out of ideas for the vast number of activities
contained in this book—very many thanks!
(Anna Jean)

Suggested songs are taken from the following song books:
Junior Praise (JP)
Mission Praise (MP)
Songs of Fellowship (SF)

CONTENTS

INTRODUCTION

For many people, both young and old, David and Goliath and the prodigal son are simply stories from long ago. We can enjoy them with very little sense of when and why they happened. But the Old Testament stories take on fresh meaning when we realize that Jesus heard them as a child. Jesus talked about shepherds, knowing that David, his ancestor, had fought savage animals to save his flock. When he talked about the prodigal son, he knew of the struggles between Jacob and Esau and Joseph and his brothers. They were his family history.

The Jewish festivals, too, were an important part of his upbringing, as they still are for children in many Jewish homes. Each one is a reminder of some important event, and a thanksgiving for one of God's many blessings. We can appreciate the Christian festivals more when we understand the link between them and the Jewish festivals.

The senses of touch, sight, hearing, smell and taste are gifts from God that our children can still enjoy. Let us use them to make the stories, and our worship, richer and more real. Don't be afraid to try something new. Keep everything fresh and exciting.

Few of us would set off on a journey of exploration without at least a map and travel guide. This book can be your guide, but you will need a Bible as your map. Read the stories for yourself, and check the Bible references. Start the journey with the first chapter of Section One ('Step into the roots of Christianity'), followed by the first chapter of Section Two ('Step into the stories of Jesus').

By learning more about Jesus' Jewish roots, we begin to gain a deeper understanding of his stories. It's an exciting journey, so enjoy taking the first few steps.

Section One

STEP INTO THE ROOTS
OF CHRISTIANITY

STEPPING-STONES
THROUGH THE AGES

START HERE Creation Flood	2000BC Abraham	1900BC Isaac	1800BC Jacob	1700BC Joseph	
					1600BC
					1500BC
	1100BC Samuel	1200BC Joshua	1300BC Moses leads exodus	1400BC	Hebrews are slaves in Egypt
1000BC Saul (first king) David (second king)					
900BC Solomon builds the temple Kingdom splits	800BC Elijah Elisha	700BC Isaiah, Jeremiah Amos, Hosea	600BC Exile to Babylon (Daniel) Jerusalem is destroyed Ezekiel EXILES RETURN	500BC	
					400BC Ezra and Nehemiah
					300BC
	AD200 Christians are persecuted	AD70 JESUS IS BORN Christian Church spreads	100BC Romans seize Jerusalem	200BC Judas Maccabeus	
AD300 Romans in Britain Christianity is established					
AD400 Patrick goes to Ireland Romans leave Britain	AD500 Columba goes to Iona Augustine comes to England	AD600	AD700	AD800 Vikings come to Britain	
					AD900 King Wenceslas is murdered
					AD1000 Normans come to Britain
	AD1400 Joan of Arc is burnt at the stake	AD1300	AD1200 Francis of Assisi	AD1100	
AD1500 The first English Bible is printed Henry VIII, Elizabeth I					
AD1600 Gunpowder plot Charles I is executed	AD1700 American independence	AD1800 Slavery is ended in the British Empire	AD1900 Two world wars People reach the moon	AD2000 A new millennium	?

A CALENDAR OF FESTIVALS

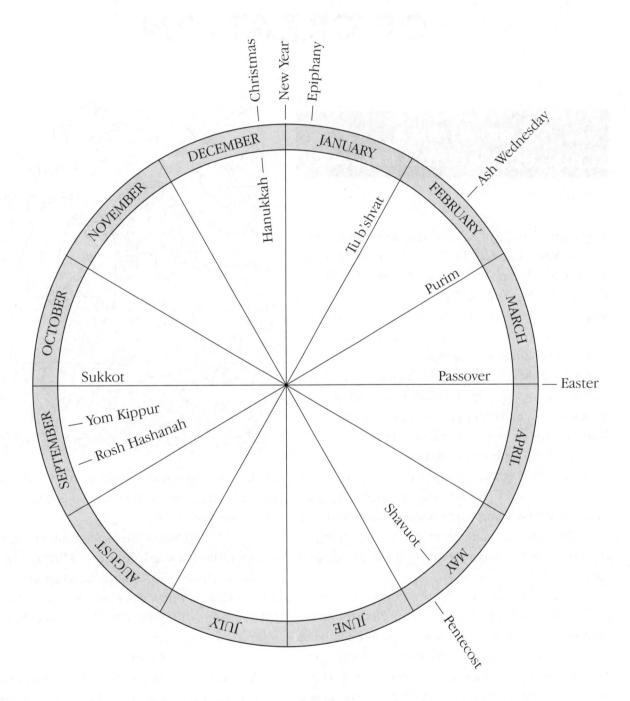

With the exception of Christmas and the western New Year, all festivals are dependent on the date of the new moon and vary from year to year.

Chapter 1

STEP INTO THE STORY OF CREATION

A GREAT IDEA... BUT HOW DO YOU BEGIN?

GENESIS 1 AND 2

The earth was formless and desolate. The raging ocean was engulfed in total darkness. Sounds gruesome, doesn't it? That's what the world was like in the beginning. Today it may be wet and windy, cold and gloomy where you are. But we know that somewhere in the world the sun is shining and birds are singing.

We wouldn't want a dark, lifeless world, and neither did God. He decided to do something about it, to make things—things to watch and listen to; things to feel, sniff, savour and enjoy. He set the whole scheme in motion.

What's the first thing you need when you decide to make something? Did you say 'light'? Exactly. That's the first thing God created. Next came the sky. Land and sea came next. It was beginning to be more like the earth we know. It was good. God said so.

Then God made food. All the fruits and grain in the world, and no one to eat it! Doesn't make sense? Think about it. If you were planning a party you'd probably wonder, 'Who shall I invite?' But your mum thinks, 'How shall I feed them?' That's what God did. He wanted everything to be ready. First he prepared the feast, then he invited the guests! It was good. God said so.

Here's some detective work for you. There's a clue in the Bible that something special is going on. Up until the animals appear, the story says, 'Then God commanded...' seven times. But after that, God uses some new words: 'Now we will make human beings; they will be like us...' *We? Us?* Who else was there?

Let's fast-forward thousands of years. In his Gospel, the apostle John says, 'Through him God made all things. Not one thing in all creation was made without him.' Yes, it was Jesus. He was there all the time! Just imagine, Father and Son doing everything together.

'How about a few more stars up here?' 'Good idea.'

'And another galaxy over there?' 'Only one?'

Yes, creation was a brilliant idea—teamwork, carefully planned.

Finally, God made Adam and Eve. He made them like himself, and he was pleased with them. He made a beautiful garden for them. He gave them power over every living creature. Now the universe was ready. And it was good. God said so.

STEP INTO THE FESTIVAL OF ROSH HASHANAH

The first day of the Jewish New Year, *Rosh Hashanah*, is a day for having fun and celebrating God's creation of the world, but it's also the first of ten 'Days of Awe' or 'Penitence'. It's a time for getting right with God—and other people. Here are some ways of keeping a personal tally for a few days.

DAYS OF PENITENCE

A TICK LIST (FOR OLDER CHILDREN)

Use a photocopy of this list and tick the items each day as you fulfil them.

Pray

❏ Talk to God. Say sorry for things you've got wrong. He'll show you what needs fixing.

Get right with others

❏ Pay your debts.
❏ If there's anything you haven't said 'thank you' for, do it now.
❏ If you've said or done anything unkind, say 'sorry'. Think of ways of making up.
❏ Have you ignored anyone who needs help? Try to find ways of helping.

Give to charity

❏ Plan a sale for a charity with your friends. Make gifts for sale. Collect (clean) second-hand clothes, toys or books.
❏ Save some of the money you usually spend on sweets and so on, and put it in a charity box.

Fast

This doesn't mean starving. There are other ways of fasting, such as:
❏ Giving up sweets or fizzy drinks.
❏ Living without your favourite TV show, pop music or computer game.

Don't boast about fasting. Just find other things to do and stay cheerful.

A BOOK OF PROMISES (FOR ANY AGE)

You will need four sheets of A4 paper.

Fold and staple the paper to make a booklet. On the front page, print your name and 'My book of promises'. Inside the book, head each page 'Day 1', 'Day 2' and so on.

Each day, pray about one thing you can promise to do, and write it down or draw a picture. It could be something to make you happier about yourself, or to make someone else happy. Give yourself a tick each night for keeping that day's promise.

STEP INTO THE SENSES

THE SENSE OF SIGHT

GOD MADE THESE

Rosh Hashanah falls about mid-September, but we can celebrate creation at any time. Read Psalm 36:5–9. Make a banner with the words 'God made these' as a heading.

> *You will need one large piece of paper, a small piece of paper for each child, paints, gold or silver paper, and scissors.*

Let each child paint one of the items mentioned in the psalm. Use gold or silver paint or paper to highlight where appropriate. Trim the pictures and paste them on to the banner. Hang it where everyone can enjoy it. Use the banner as a prayer focus (see page 18).

OUR FIRST HOME—PAINT IT!

Think about these verses from Psalm 90:1–2: 'O Lord, you have always been our home. Before you created the hills or brought the world into being, you were eternally God, and will be God for ever.'

Imagine what 'home' might have been before God made the world. Would we have been floating on some kind of cloud, or on another planet? Paint your picture, but no cheating—rockets and spacesuits hadn't been invented!

HAPPY NEW YEAR!

Make cards to celebrate the Jewish New Year.

> *For each, you will need a piece of stiff, coloured card, smaller pieces of white card, scissors, crayons or paints, fine thread, Sellotape, and a marker pen.*

Cut the cards in advance. Let the children write the message, then colour and cut out the planets and stars, with a large curve for the sun. Attach a thread to each with Sellotape, then on the inside of the card, covering the ends with a strip of Sellotape.

sun — cut out

THE SENSE OF SOUND

ARE YOU ALIVE?

Are you sure you're alive?

> *You will need a stethoscope and a tape recorder with microphone.*

Hold the stethoscope to your chest and listen to your heartbeat. Now hold the microphone of the tape recorder against your chest and press 'Record'. Play it back and listen to your heartbeat. Try it on your friends, and at home on family and pets.

Now drink some water and listen to your tummy. Amazing, isn't it?

MUSIC AND MOVEMENT

You will need a tape recording of parts of Gustav Holst's Planets Suite.

Talk about the planets and what they represent in legend—for example, Venus, the bringer of peace; Jupiter, bringer of jollity; Mercury, the winged messenger; and Uranus, the magician. Let the children move and dance to the music.

THE CALL OF THE SHOFAR

The ram's horn (*shofar*) is blown a hundred times at *Rosh Hashanah* to call the people to turn away from wrongdoing and towards God. It reminds them of the ram that God gave Abraham to sacrifice instead of his son.

Make your own *shofar*.

You will need a piece of heavy-duty A4 paper, some washproof surgical tape, Sellotape, rubber band and pencil.

Practise on pieces of old paper. Wind one corner of the paper around a pencil, and roll it to form a cone shape. When it's about right, slide a rubber

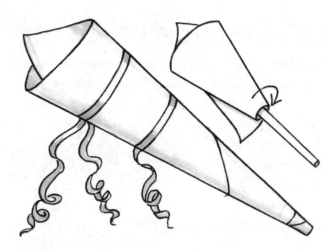

band over it to hold it in place. Remove the pencil, and wrap about 5cm of washproof tape around the end of the cone. This will form a clean mouthpiece. Use Sellotape to hold the rest in shape. You could decorate your *shofar* with coloured streamers.

IF I WERE A BUTTERFLY

Sing this song together (JP 94).

THE SENSE OF TOUCH

YES, I'M ALIVE

There are two places where you can feel your own pulse easily. One is on the inside of your wrist, below the base of the thumb. The other is at the side of your neck, below the ear.

Lay your fingers against these spots until you feel the beat. Try testing your pulse before exercising. Try again five minutes later. It should speed up, and then slow down again.

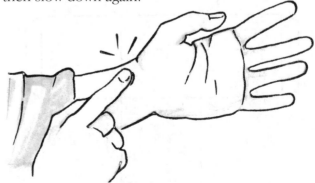

HOW BIG ARE YOU?

Compare your size to the biggest things in nature. Here are some approximate heights and lengths:

Bamboo: 37m
Anaconda: 9.15m
Sunflower: 3m
Blue whale: 27.5m
Crocodile: 6m
Californian redwood tree: 92m

If possible, lay yourselves out end to end to find how many of you equal one of these things. If you don't have enough space for that, use a calculator to find out how many times taller or longer these things are than yourself.

GIFT BOXES

Rosh Hashanah is one of several times when it's traditional to give presents. Use this basic pattern for making boxes, changing the shape and size to suit your purpose (for example, a large, shallow one for cakes; a tall, narrow one for the spice box on page 78).

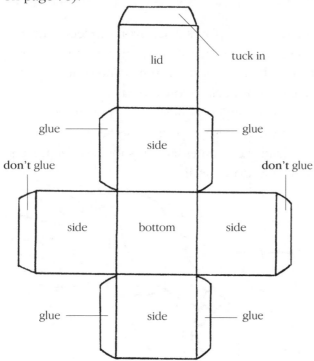

THE SENSE OF SMELL

A SWEET NEW YEAR

There's nothing like the smell of freshly baked bread. At *Rosh Hashanah* it is traditional to bake rounded loaves of *challah* bread to represent the kind of New Year that everyone prays for. The shape signifies the continuation of life.

To make the bread, you will need:
- *700g plain flour (sifted), 1 teaspoon salt, and 1 packet easy-blend yeast, all mixed together.*
- *100g sugar, dissolved in 250 ml warm water, added to above.*
- *100g oil and 2 large eggs, mixed into dough.*
- *A few dried raisins or sultanas to be added.*

1. Mix the dough, then divide it into 4–8 pieces. Let the pieces rise for up to 2 hours.
2. Let each children knead and shape a piece of dough into a circular bun, starting with a fat sausage.
3. Put the dough into a pre-heated oven at 200°C/Gas Mark 6. After one minute, reduce to 180°C/Gas Mark 5, and bake for 30–45 minutes.

Safety tip: Follow all necessary safety precautions, and do not allow very young children to touch a hot stove or baking tray.

LAVENDER BAGS

Make lavender bags for your charity sale or as gifts. Ask people for lavender from their gardens. Look for remnants of lace curtaining in a sale.

You will need circles of net 25cm in diameter, about 40cm of fancy cord or thick coloured wool, a darning needle, pinking shears and dried lavender.

1. Cut out a circle of net.
2. Trim the edge with pinking shears.

3. Thread the cord with big running stitches, a generous thumb-width away from the edge.
4. Put a heap of dried lavender in the centre of the circle.
5. Pull the thread tight and knot it, knotting the two ends so that it can be hung from a coathanger in the wardrobe.

THE SENSE OF TASTE

SOMETHING TO GIVE

Make honey cakes, either to sell for fund-raising or give as gifts.

You will need:
- *85g each margarine and sugar, creamed together well.*
- *2 beaten eggs and 115g honey, added to above.*
- *225g self-raising flour, sifted and mixed in gently.*

If this mixture is too stiff, add a little milk. Spoon into about 15 bun tins lined with paper cases. Cook for 15–20 minutes at 190°C/Gas Mark 5.

Make pretty gift boxes for the honey cakes.

CARROT TZIMMES

'Tzimmes' means almost any kind of stew, whether fruit, vegetable or meat. But in this one the carrots represent sweetness. The word for 'carrot' in Hebrew means 'to increase', so when you eat carrots you are praying for many blessings. Enjoy this carrot stew.

You will need:
- *4 onions, clove garlic, 6 carrots, 1 parsnip, 4 potatoes.*
- *6 prunes, 150ml orange juice, half a lemon (sliced), 2 tsp honey.*
- *1 tsp cinnamon, 3 cloves, 1 vegetable stock cube, 300ml water.*

Let the older children do the cutting, and the younger ones the cleaning, measuring and mixing. Slice the carrots so that they look like coins. Cut the other vegetables into chunks, and mix all the ingredients in a casserole. Add more water to cover the ingredients if necessary. Cover. Cook at about 170°/Gas Mark 4 for an hour or longer.

MAKE YOUR OWN MUESLI

Did you know that muesli was the first food created? God said, 'Let the earth produce all kinds of plants, those that bear grain and those that bear fruit…' (Genesis 1:11). From the following basic recipe, the children can make their own mixture.

You will need:
- *170g rolled oats, 50g wheat flakes, 40g bran.*
- *175g fruit (raisins or sultanas, chopped dried apricots, prunes, bananas, apples).*
- *50g sunflower seeds, 150g chopped nuts (beware of peanut allergies).*

Enjoy this mixture with milk and perhaps a little honey.

STEP INTO PRAYER

SHARING AND PRAYING

You will need liquid honey and slices of apple.

It is traditional to dip pieces of apple into honey and enjoy them on *Rosh Hashanah*. Let the children sit in an informal circle. Begin by thanking God for his goodness, and for giving this opportunity to celebrate together.

The children pass the bowl of honey around, handing a piece of apple to the next person and saying 'Thank you, God, for… [name]. May he/she have a sweet New Year.' They then dip the apple in the honey before handing it on to the next person.

GOD'S CONSTANT LOVE

Read Psalm 36:5–9. Discuss the created things mentioned. What senses do we need to appreciate them? Make a list and thank God for them. Pray for those whose senses are impaired. If you have made the banner on page 14, use it to focus your thoughts.

CLAP YOUR HANDS

During *Rosh Hashanah*, Psalm 47 is repeated seven times. Read it now, as a prayer, clapping and using shakers at the end of each verse, with cheers in verse 5. (See page 70 for shakers.)

HANNAH'S PRAYER

Read Hannah's story from 1 Samuel 1:9–18. It is traditional to read this in the synagogue at *Rosh Hashanah*. As Hannah prayed silently, so can we. Invite the children to imitate Hannah and ask for something privately, for themselves or someone else. End with Eli's blessing: 'Go in peace, and may the God of Israel give you what you have asked him for.'

Chapter 2

STEP INTO THE STORY OF DISOBEDIENCE

JUST TRUST ME

GENESIS 3 AND 4

Close your eyes. You're in a wildlife park. There's every animal that ever lived, including some you've never heard of. None of them will hurt you. You can stroke the lions and swim with the crocodiles. You can swing from the treetops with the apes. You can have pterodactyl races. There's rainforest and pasture, snow on the mountain tops, and honey bees. God is there with you. He made it all, including you. He makes a special friend for you. Sometimes he leaves you alone. Sometimes he keeps you company. Yes, this is the Garden of Eden, and the friends are Adam and Eve.

All new things come with a warning, have you noticed? You get your first bike and they tell you, 'Don't go on the main road.' You go to your first party and they tell you, 'Don't make yourself sick.' This great wildlife park is like that. There's just one fruit you mustn't eat, or you'll die—just one. God told Adam, Adam told Eve, and Eve told the snake.

The snake said, 'Rubbish. It's not true.'

So who did they believe, the snake or God? Yes, that's right—the snake. After they'd eaten the fruit, they probably argued something like this:

'It's all your fault.'

'No, it isn't. He told me…'

'Yes, but you said…'

'But if you hadn't…'

'Well, how did I know?'

Sounds familiar, doesn't it?

God had warned Adam and Eve that they would die, but he loved them. He didn't want to lose them. So he let them live until they were old, but they had to leave the Garden of Eden. They had to work hard for the rest of their lives. They would feel pain. They hadn't trusted God, so how could they trust one another?

Adam and Eve had two sons. Abel was a shepherd, a good-natured boy. He gave God his first new lamb. Cain was a farmer, but a bad-tempered one. He gave God 'some' of his crops. God didn't like his attitude. God warned him, 'Sin is crouching at your door. It wants to rule you, but you must overcome it.' Cain didn't listen. He murdered his brother instead.

First disobedience, then murder. But God never gives up. He loves us too much.

19

STEP INTO THE FESTIVAL OF YOM KIPPUR

THREE BOOKS

Yom Kippur, the tenth day after *Rosh Hashanah*, is called 'the Sabbath of Sabbaths'. It is the most solemn day of the year. Tradition says that God opens three books on this day. The Book of Death is for very wicked people. The Book of Life is for those who are good. The third is for the 'don't-know-yets'. The aim is to have your name in God's 'good' book before it closes on *Yom Kippur*.

- Jonah sulked. He refused to help. Can we think of times we've been like Jonah?
- What did God do about it?

JONAH'S STORY

This difference has been suggested between Jews and Christians: the Jews teach their children that they were created to succeed, whereas Christians emphasize the burden of sin. Children need to know that God created us for success, not failure. We may turn away from him, but his love brings us back to him time and time again.

Jonah's story is read at *Yom Kippur* every year during the afternoon service.

You'll find the story of Jonah in the book named after him in the Old Testament. It is quite a short story, just four chapters long. Read the story from your Bible, or from a children's Bible or Bible storybook, and think about these things:

- God went to a lot of trouble to warn not only the Jews, but people who didn't love him. Can we think of people today who help others whether they like them or not? (Suggestions might be doctors and firemen.) How many can you count?

TRUE OR FALSE?

Read out each of the following statements, and ask the children to put their hands up if they think it is true. (If you have lots of space, they could run one way for 'True', the other for 'False'.) Discuss each question before going on to the next.

- God told Adam and Eve, 'Do whatever you want to do.'
- The snake said, 'You must do as God tells you.'
- Abel said, 'I don't want this old sheep: God can have it.'
- Cain said, 'God won't mind if it isn't my very best.'
- God said, 'Thank you, Cain, that's just what I wanted.'
- Eve said, 'Get away, snake, you're telling lies.'
- Cain said, 'I don't know where my brother is.'
- God said, 'You didn't trust me. Now you'll have to work hard for a living.'

STEP INTO THE SENSES

THE SENSE OF SIGHT

THAT SNAKE!

In the story, the snake is used as a symbol of the thing that spoiled things for everyone. Make a snake up a tree in the Garden of Eden.

You will need a small branch from a dead tree, a plant pot with soil or pebbles, green paper cut from the pattern below, marker pens and shiny patches.

Plant the branch in the pot. Cut out your snake, decorate it and wind it through the 'branches'. Add paper cut-outs of fruit if you like.

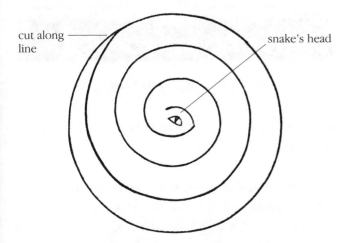

cut along line

snake's head

WHERE'S JONAH?

See Jonah disappearing inside the fish. Make this card to give as a present.

You will need pieces of firm card, colouring materials and glue.

fold (do not cut)

cut out and discard shaded areas

glue paper spring to body and fish

inside the fish

Cut out the shapes and follow the diagrams to make your card. An older person may need to help with the cutting. Colour it in and write your greeting inside.

A FEAST OF WORDS

At *Yom Kippur*, a day of fasting, the scrolls of the Torah are laid on the table in place of food. Make your Bible look special for this day by making a cover for it.

You will need a piece of quality paper big enough to wrap around your Bible, with flaps to tuck inside the covers, and small pieces of plain paper. (Look for remnants of rich-looking paper in a wallpaper shop.)

To decorate your Bible, you could cut out the shapes of the two tablets of the law that Moses brought down from Sinai (see picture on page 47), or some other symbol. A tree? A flame? Whatever you choose, cut out the shapes carefully and paste them firmly to the front cover, allowing them to dry before you cover your Bible.

fold over back and front covers of Bible

THE SENSE OF SOUND

THE TRUMPET CALL

Trumpets are used as a warning signal, or to announce an important visitor. Why do you think the trumpet is a good instrument to use for these occasions? If possible, invite someone to play examples, such as *Reveille* and *The Last Post*. Or listen to a recording of the introduction to 'The trumpet shall sound' from Handel's *Messiah*.

WRITE YOUR OWN STORY

Here are some alarm sounds:
- A fire alarm, a car horn, police, ambulance or ship's siren.
- A dog barks, the doorbell or telephone rings, someone screams.
- The oven timer pings, an alarm clock rings.

Can you think of any others? Work in small groups and make up a story entitled 'A day I will never forget', bringing in as many alarms as you can. You have ten minutes.

Each group can tell their story to the others, with a chief storyteller from each group. There could be a prize for the group with the most alarms.

A STORM AT SEA

Fill large plastic water or milk containers about a quarter full of water. Screw the lids on. Make the kind of sounds Jonah might have heard by swishing the water first slowly, then more quickly, and then slowly again.

THE SHOFAR

The beginning and end of every activity can be announced with the call of the *shofar*. Instructions for making one are on page 15.

THE SENSE OF TOUCH

RAW MATERIALS

Identify some of the things Adam and Eve found outside Eden.

You will need a number of large brown paper bags with one of these things inside each of them:
- *stones*
- *eggshells (washed)*
- *gravel*
- *large seeds*
- *twigs*
- *a gardening fork and trowel*
- *soil*
- *sand*

Let the children take turns to identify what they can feel inside each bag—eyes closed, of course. How might these things have seemed different to Adam and Eve once they had left Eden? How would Adam and Eve have to work with them now?

BAD HABITS

You will need a reel of tacking cotton.

Break off a couple of metres of tacking cotton. Ask a volunteer to stand with his arms at his side, and tie the cotton around him below the elbow, knotting it firmly. Ask him to break his arms free. Easy!

Break off a length that will go round about six times. Ask the volunteer to try breaking free again. Is it still easy? Now use the whole of the reel. This time it should be much harder. What does this tell us about things that we do wrong over and over again? Now think about the heading, 'Bad habits'. Remember, God gives us freedom: we can choose *not* to give in to those bad habits every time.

ROUGH CUSTOMERS

Paint three-dimensional pictures.

You will need large sheets of stiff paper, pieces of corrugated card and/or polystyrene, shiny paper, scissors, glue and paints.

Read Job 40:15–24 and 41:12–34. What animals do Behemoth and Leviathan remind you of? Paint pictures of them, but make them three-dimensional. Paste layers of board or polystyrene to make Behemoth's muscles stand out. Make his tail from cord. Cut out rough, shiny scales for Leviathan. Use empty boxes and packages for materials.

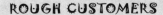

THE SENSE OF SMELL

SMELLS FISHY

Read the story of Jonah, which is read during the afternoon service on *Yom Kippur*. Yes, God cared about the people that Jonah didn't like, and gave them a chance to get right with him.

You will need samples of fish to smell (suggestions: pickled herrings, kippers, fish paste, tinned sardines, fresh fish).

Cover each dish with a clean cloth and let the children try to identify them by smell. Which one would you most hate to smell if you were Jonah?

Try samples of the cooked fish (assuming they are fresh) on crackers.

WHAT WENT WRONG?

When we buy food in the shops, it usually has a 'sell by' date on the packet. Why is it important for our food to be fresh?

Arrange these things on a tray—some fresh fruit and flowers, a glass of milk, a slice of bread, a piece of cheese. Smells lovely, doesn't it? Cover the tray to keep the flies away, and leave overnight. Smell it again the next day, and the one after that. Discuss what's happening, and what, if anything, we can do about it.

THE SENSE OF TASTE

A SAD TASTE

With so many hungry people in the world, it is important to think about wastage, and how we spoil the good things God gives us.

> *You will need a plate of plain biscuits which have become stale and soggy (but not mouldy!), a bottle of cold tea or coffee with a pinch of salt.*

All the things on the plate look OK. Let everyone taste them. Talk about what has gone wrong. The biscuits can be thrown out for the birds, and the drink poured away.

THE TASTE OF WATER

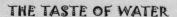

Imagine you are in a desert, and you are very, very thirsty. Now someone brings a tray with sparkling glasses and a large jug of cool, fresh water. Listen to the water as it is poured into the glass. Take it in your hands. Close your eyes and sip the water slowly. Think of words to describe how it feels on your lips, on your tongue and in your throat. Does it really taste of nothing?

BREAK YOUR FAST... BUT REMEMBER

> *You will need bread and apricot jam.*

The forbidden fruit eaten by Adam and Eve may have been an apricot. *Yom Kippur* is a day of total fasting, and on that day everyone wears white. We can remind ourselves of *Yom Kippur* and the story of Adam and Eve by having a modest breakfast of bread spread with apricot jam. Enjoy it, but at the same time think about what it represents.

STEP INTO PRAYER

A NEW YEAR PRAYER

The following prayer was said by the high priest in the most sacred place, the Holy of Holies. Print these lines separately on numbered pieces of card.

May it be your will, God,
Our God, and the God of our fathers,
that this year, which has come upon us
and upon all of your people Israel
wherever they may be,
may be a year of light,
a year of blessing,
a year of joy,
a year of pleasure,
a year of glory.

Give the cards out, the shorter ones to the younger children. Let them read their section in turn, helping the younger ones if necessary. Repeat this a few times, inviting the children to join in with any of the words they have memorized.

A SILENT PRAYER

You will need a pebble for each child, and a large bucket or bowl with some water in it.

Put some waterproof sheeting underneath the bucket or bowl. There is a tradition of throwing pebbles, representing things we're sorry for, into the sea or a stream. Give a pebble to each person, explaining what it represents. They hold it in their hands, close their eyes, and think of something they want to say 'sorry' for to God. They imagine the wrong thing inside the pebble. When they are ready, they throw their pebble into the water. As they do so, they can say, 'Sorry, God. Thank you that I can leave this with you.'

Finally, say the following prayer together:

Thank you, God, for hearing our silent prayers. Thank you for forgiving us. Amen.

If possible, take out the pebbles and pour the water away where everyone can watch.

Pieces of bread are sometimes used instead of pebbles.

STEP INTO THE STORY OF A NEW START

THE FIRST BOAT-BUILDER

People didn't make a very good start, did they? First they didn't trust God, then they invented murder. They thought up new—and worse—ways of being wicked. After ten generations, the world was full of wickedness. God said, 'I will wipe out these people I have created, and also the animals and birds, because I am sorry that I made any of them.'

But there was one man who talked to God and trusted him. His name was Noah. We can find his story in the book of Genesis in the Old Testament, chapters 6—9. The Bible says, 'Noah had no faults and was the only good man of his time. He lived in fellowship with God' (Genesis 6:9–10). When Noah was born, his father said, 'From the very ground on which the Lord put a curse, this child will bring us relief from all our hard work' (Genesis 5:29).

God told Noah, 'I am going to send a flood on the earth to destroy every living being.' Noah had to build a boat to save himself, his family and enough animals to start again. Yes, because Noah was good, God saved his family, too.

There's a song that goes, 'The animals went in two by two', but Noah was allowed seven pairs of the edible ones. He had exactly seven days to build the ark and get everything ready. Talk about hard work! And when they'd all climbed (or flown) on board, guess who closed the door? God did. He just couldn't resist touching that boat!

The water rose, and every living creature was drowned. But Noah's boat stayed afloat for more than a year. One day Noah opened a window and sent out a raven. It circled the boat. Then he sent out a dove. It flew back. A week later he tried again. Back it came with a fresh olive leaf in its beak, a sign of new life! The third time it stayed away.

Very soon they reached land. God told Noah, 'Go out of the boat with your wife, your sons, and their wives. Take all the birds and animals out with you, so that they may reproduce and spread all over the earth.'

After they'd stepped on to dry land, the first thing Noah did was to build an altar and say 'thank you' to God. God blessed Noah. He promised Noah that he would never flood the earth again. But there must be no more killing. God showed Noah a rainbow in the sky. He told Noah, 'That is the sign of the promise which I am making to all living beings.'

The rainbow is still God's sign of his promise to Noah—and to us.

STEP INTO THE FESTIVAL OF SUKKOT

SUKKOT: THE FEAST OF SHELTERS

Leviticus 23:42 says, 'All the people of Israel shall live in shelters for seven days.' Deuteronomy 16:14 says, 'Enjoy it.'

Sukkot—or Tabernacles—is an autumn harvest festival. It reminds people of the forty years when the people of Israel wandered in the desert. The theme is one of rejoicing, sleeping under the stars and giving hospitality.

Make your own *sukkah*, which means 'shelter' or 'booth'. Ideally, it should be outdoors, open to the stars, and big enough to stand up and move around in. However, you can make an indoor version with a little imagination.

You will need two or more clothes horses propped against the wall, tied firmly together, with bamboo poles across the top to make a 'roof'.

bamboo

Hang old sheets or curtains on your *sukkah* for walls. Now decorate it with as much greenery as you can, including fruit and vegetables. If real foliage isn't available, make paper chains and streamers, and hang pictures. Put mats and cushions on the floor.

Use your *sukkah* as a place for prayer, Bible reading and meals.

WHAT DID THE NEIGHBOURS SAY?

Read Genesis 6:9–21. While Noah was busy building his ark, what do you think the other people said about him? What would the children say as they watched? What would their parents say?

Perform your own drama, some playing the parts of Noah and his family, others the neighbours.

SIMCHAT TORAH

Torah means the first five books of the Bible, which tell the story up to the death of Moses. *Simchat Torah* means 'rejoicing in the Torah (or law)'. This festival, which is held on the last day of *Sukkot*, was not celebrated until the tenth century, but today it is a time of great rejoicing. The scrolls of the *Torah* are paraded, with singing, dancing, flags, streamers, and throwing of sweets.

Think of ways in which we can rejoice in our Bible. Find out about the work of the International Bible Society, and how many people still do not have a Bible in their own language.

STEP INTO THE SENSES

THE SENSE OF SIGHT

GOD'S PROMISE

Make a mosaic poster of the rainbow.

> *You will need a large sheet of plain paper, transparent paper in red, orange, yellow, green and blue, some scissors and pots of paste.*

Outline the arcs of the rainbow on the paper. Print a heading, 'God's promise', across the top. Let the children cut the transparent paper into squares about 2cm wide. Accuracy is not essential. Let them paste these squares on, to fill the spaces on the paper. Encourage co-operation and teamwork. Some can paste while others are still cutting.

Display the poster where it will have maximum impact.

DECORATE YOUR SUKKAH

The *sukkah* is going to be your 'home' for a few days, so hang some pictures on the 'walls'.

Paint pictures of ten different things God has made to beautify the world—the heavens, skies, mountains, sea, people, animals, birds, food, water, light. Paste the pictures on to a firm backing, then attach cords and hang them on the *sukkah* walls.

THE SENSE OF SOUND

GOOD OLD NOAH HAD AN ARK

Sing Noah's version of 'Old McDonald had a farm', with the words, 'Good old Noah had an ark, ee-i-ee-i-o, and in that ark he had some…'.

Make your own list of animals, and have fun working out the sounds they make.

CARNIVAL OF THE ANIMALS

Make a tape recording of some of the pieces from Saint-Saens' *Carnival of the Animals* (suggestions: Lion, Elephant, Aquarium, Long Ears and Aviary). Ask the children to guess which animal each tune represents. Explore how each animal moves.

A thought: would there have been any fishes inside the ark?

SONGS TO ENJOY

Have lots of fun making up the actions—and dance the following songs.

'Rise, and shine, and give God his glory, glory' (JP210)
'God is good' (JP55)

Make coloured flags to enjoy with these and other songs.

DEDICATED TO THE LORD

In Zechariah 14:20, the prophet said that at *Sukkot* even the horse's harness bells should be dedicated to the Lord. Tie bells to your ankles and wrists as you sing and dance.

THE SENSE OF TOUCH

THE WHOLE BODY

During the *Simchat Torah* celebrations, a bundle of plants called the *lulav* is held in the right hand and waved in all directions. This represents worshipping God with the whole body.

The plants are:
- Palm: a symbol of Israel and victory. It also represents the spine.
- Willow: represents the mouth.
- Myrtle: represents the eyes.

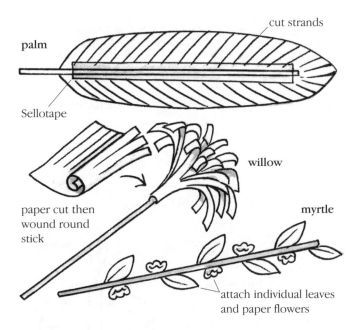

In their left hand, people held a kind of citrus fruit, the *etrog*, to represent the heart. The myrtle has sweet-smelling flowers.

> *You will need green canes from a garden shop, green paper, white or pink tissue paper, and Sellotape.*

Cut leaves as illustrated above and fix to canes with Sellotape.

ALL ABOARD!

For a large project, make a model of the ark using large boxes, with windows cut in the sides, and let the children make model animals from playdough or plasticine. A detachable sloped roof can be held in place with Blu-tack. Make the 'sea' with screwed-up blue and green tissue paper.

THE SENSE OF SMELL

A FRAGRANT DWELLING

Find sweet-smelling plants to weave into the fabric of your booth (suggestions: lavender, rosemary and pine). Ask for help at a garden centre or florists' shop.

NOT SO FRAGRANT

Think about a visit you might have made to a zoo or a farm. Talk about how the animals smelt. Which was the smelliest? Try to arrange a trip and notice the smells.

A POMANDER

Pomanders have been used for thousands of years in various forms. The word means 'box of perfumes', but you can make one to hang in your *sukkah*, and later at home.

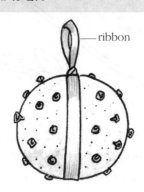
ribbon

> *You will need a small orange, several cloves, a length of narrow green ribbon, and cocktail sticks.*

Make holes in the orange skin using a cocktail stick. Stick the cloves into the holes, and tie the ribbon round the orange, making a loop to hang it. Your pomander will give a refreshing smell for a long time.

THE SENSE OF TASTE

PARTY TIME

Invite someone from outside your group to a feast. Traditional recipes for *Sukkot* include things made of fruit and nuts. Use your imagination, or make these apple puffs.

> *You will need:*
> * *A pack of frozen puff pastry, rolled very thinly and cut into 8cm squares.*
> * *450g cooking apples, peeled and grated.*
> * *55g each sultanas, cake crumbs and sugar.*
> * *1 lemon, 1 teaspoon cinnamon, 1 beaten egg.*

Younger children can peel apples with a potato peeler, crumble the cake, grate apple and lemon rind and do the mixing. Older ones can roll the pastry out very thinly and cut into approximately 10cm squares.

Sprinkle the squares with cake crumbs. Grate the lemon rind and squeeze the juice of half of it. Mix all ingredients thoroughly, and place a spoonful of mixture on each square. Paint the edges with beaten egg, fold to make triangles, and glaze the tops with beaten egg.

Place on a lightly greased tray. Bake in a hot oven (200°C/Gas Mark 6) for about ten minutes.

Warning: the filling will be very hot. Allow plenty of time to cool down before eating. Don't give nuts to very young children or anyone who has a nut allergy.

RECIPE ADAPTED FROM ONE IN MARGOT R. HODSON'S *A FEAST OF SEASONS*

GIFT BAGS

A bag of sugared almonds is given as a gift in many cultures. Make smaller versions of the lavender bags on page 16 and fill them with three or four sugared almonds or dried fruit and nuts. To make them even simpler, cut 22cm squares of net, put the almonds inside, hold the net by the corners and slip a small rubber band over them. When the 'frills' are arranged prettily, tie a bow of ribbon to cover the rubber band.

STEP INTO PRAYER

GIVING ALL TO GOD

Read Psalm 9:1–2. If you have made the *lulav*, use it now; otherwise do the movements without it.

Stand or sit quietly, holding the *lulav*. If you do not have a citrus fruit to represent the *etrog*, hold out your left hand. As the children repeat each line, let them point to the appropriate plant or body part.

I will praise you, Lord, with all my heart.
(etrog = heart)

I will tell of all the wonderful things you have done. (palm = spine)

I will sing with joy because of you.
(willow = mouth)

I will sing praise to you, Almighty God.
(myrtle = eyes)

Ask the children what wonderful things God has done in their lives, or in the world, that they would like to thank him for. Thank him for bodies we can use for his purposes. Pray for those whose bodies are disabled in any way, but who can still praise God.

A DAY OF LIGHT

After the loud celebrations, use this as a time of quiet, reflective prayer.

> *You will need 16 tea-lights, four plates, and matches.*

One day during *Sukkot*, the women's court in the temple was lit with four lamps in each corner, each lamp with four flames. Remember that Jesus said, 'I am the light of the world' in the temple (John 8:12).

Put a plate with four tea-lights in each corner of the room. Sit down quietly, and take turns to read Psalm 117. This, the shortest psalm, is one of six read during *Sukkot*.

PRAY FOR RAIN

Sukkot is the last festival before the winter rains. On the last day, the priest would fetch water in a gold pitcher from the Pool of Siloam outside Jerusalem, and pour it over the altar while the people prayed for rain. This was the day when Jesus said, in the temple, 'Whoever is thirsty should come to me' (John 7:37).

Pray for all who need rain and clean water—and Jesus.

Chapter 4

STEP INTO THE STORY OF A FAMILY

ONE BIG FAMILY

GENESIS 11—50

Abraham, Isaac and Jacob were three very special people. They weren't perfect. They told lies and they cheated. But they did one important thing: they listened to God.

Some people like to explore their family tree. Perhaps they're related to royalty—or a highwayman. Jesus' family tree is right at the beginning of Matthew's Gospel. It goes right back to Abraham.

God wanted people to spread all over the earth. But after Noah they stayed put. They became cruel and selfish, so God decided to try again. He would create a family to spread across the world and last for ever.

God told Abraham, 'I will make you into a great nation and I will bless you.' But there was one big problem. God told Abraham that he would have a son, but he was nearly a hundred years old, and Sarah, his wife, was far too old to have children. You can't blame her for laughing! Well, God kept his promise, and their son's name, Isaac, means 'he laughs'.

When God told Abraham to sacrifice Isaac, his son, Abraham trusted God and started to obey, but before he could use the knife, God gave him a ram to sacrifice in place of the boy.

Isaac grew up and married his cousin Rebecca. She travelled by camel to meet him, her gold bracelets and nose ring gleaming in the sunlight. It was love at first sight.

Isaac and Rebecca had twin boys, Esau and Jacob. Esau was born first, so he should have been Number One son, but Rebecca helped Jacob to cheat and become Number One son instead. Esau was furious, and threatened to murder his brother. Jacob fled.

Jacob married two of his cousins, the sisters Leah and Rachel. They were jealous of each other. They had many children, and they had lots of adventures.

Jacob wanted God's blessing so badly that he wrestled with God. In the wrestling match his hip was pulled out of joint, and he limped for the rest of his life. But God did bless him, and gave him the new name of 'Israel', which means 'he perseveres with God'. His sons became the leaders of the twelve tribes of Israel.

Many years later, the apostle Paul wrote, 'Those who believe are children of Abraham.' If we follow Jesus we're part of Abraham's family, too. Jesus' forefathers weren't all perfect. But they were part of God's promise, and so are we.

STEP INTO THE FESTIVAL OF TU B'SHVAT

NEW YEAR FOR TREES

Tu b'shvat is a yearly festival in Israel. New trees are planted in the early spring. Jewish people in other parts of the world send money to pay for them. Schoolchildren plant them and say a special blessing.

The book of Leviticus laid down the rules telling Jewish people how to live. In Leviticus 25:23 they were told, 'Your land must not be sold on a permanent basis, because you do not own it; it belongs to God, and you are like foreigners who are allowed to make use of it.'

There are many rules for keeping the land healthy and fruitful. One is that the land must have a 'Sabbath' rest every seven years. Fruits were not to be eaten for three years after tree planting. That gave the tree time to establish itself. In the fourth year, the people offered the fruit to God. Only in the fifth year could they eat the fruit.

Get in touch with your nearest Forestry Department or local authorities; find out if there's a tree-planting scheme you could take part in.

THE LAW OF THE LAND

Read Leviticus 25:18–19: 'Obey all the Lord's laws and commands, so that you may live in safety in the land. The land will produce its crops, and you will have all you want to eat and will live in safety.'

What rules do we have about taking care of the land? Are they good rules? Can you think of better rules that you would like to make?

FAMILY STORIES

There is not enough space in this book to tell all the stories of Abraham's amazing family, but you can read them for yourselves. In the Bible, a children's Bible, or Bible storybook, look for stories about:
- Abraham's long journeys.
- The time Abraham almost sacrificed his son.
- Isaac's meeting with Rebecca.
- The birth of their twins, Jacob and Esau.
- Joseph's dreams, how he ended up in Egypt, and… well, just look on your library shelves.

STEP INTO THE SENSES

THE SENSE OF SIGHT

A FAMILY TREE

If we go through the story carefully, we can draw a family tree, starting with Abraham. Start by reading Matthew 1:1–2. Now look at Genesis 35:22–26. Here you will find the names of Jacob's twelve sons. Which of Jacob's sons carries on the family name? Check in Genesis 49:22–26. Draw a picture of the family tree and put the names in the right places. How many people can you fill in from the different stories you read about Abraham and his family?

OASIS

Imagine Abraham's family travelling through the desert, and make an oasis for them.

You will need a large tray or shallow cardboard box, some sand, a mirror or piece of glass for the pool, and palm trees made of green paper, following the instructions for the willow branches on page 29.

Now make a family—as big as you like—with plasticine. You can dress them with scraps of light fabric. Make tents for them, and camels, goats and sheep. (Animals are easier to model if they are lying down!)

JACOB'S SHEEP

Jacob played tricks to make sure he got the best sheep. Read about it in Genesis 30:25–43.

To make a sheep like Jacob's, you will need an empty cotton reel, 3 pipe cleaners about 12cm long, scraps of white paper, cotton wool, paste, Sellotape and a black marker pen.

To make the sheep, shape the head with a cotton wool ball, and wrap cotton wool around the body, neck, tail and legs, gluing where needed. Glue on paper ears. Dot the sheep with black speckles and two eyes.

THE SENSE OF SOUND

FATHER ABRAHAM

Sing the following song, just for fun. Add a new movement after each verse:

> *Father Abraham had many sons,*
> *Many sons had Father Abraham.*
> [count on your fingers]
> *I am one of them, and so are you,*
> [point to self and someone else]
> *So let's all praise the Lord.* [wave hands high]

> *Stand up… clap hands… turn around…*
> *stamp your feet, and so on.*

SHOUTS OF JOY

Read Psalm 96:11–13.

Sing 'You shall go out with joy' (MP281).

PEACE UNTO YOU

Sing the song 'Hevenu, shalom' (JP81).

Shalom means many things, including peace, good health and happiness. The traditional greeting 'shalom alechem' is answered with 'alechem shalom'. (You don't pronounce the 'c' in *alechem*.)

Father Abraham

Composer: Unknown

THE SENSE OF TOUCH

IT MAKES SENSE

Read Isaiah 28:23–29. Do your own experiment.

> *You will need a chopping board, a wooden mallet, pestle and mortar, dill or cumin seeds.*

Sprinkle the seeds on the board, and beat them with the hammer. What happens? Do you end up with the kind of powder you could use for cooking? Now try with a small pestle and mortar. It makes sense, doesn't it?

JACOB AND HIS SONS

You can read the full story of Isaac and Esau in Genesis 27. Esau and Isaac were very different. One was hairy, the other smooth. One was a hunter and the other a stay-at-home. They felt and smelled differently.

> *You will need a variety of fabrics (for example, smooth satin, rough tweed, lace, denim, knitted wool) and a bag to conceal them in.*

Blindfold the children, and let them each take a piece of fabric out of the bag. They must decide what kind of person would wear that fabric. Would they be young or old, rich or poor, and so on? Why would a person wear certain things at one time and not another?

LEAF RUBBING

> *You will need firm, clean leaves from mature trees, some soft paper and wax crayons.*

Choose some leaves. Lay them on a board and cover them with paper. Rub over the leaves using the side of the crayon, stroking one way only. You will soon see a 'picture' of the leaf appear. Make a display on a poster, writing the name of the leaf below each one.

WHAT KIND OF TREE?

In Isaiah 41:19 God says to the people, 'I will make cedars grow in the desert, and acacias and myrtles and olive trees. Forests will grow in barren land, forests of pine and juniper and cypress.' When King Solomon built the temple he used many different types of wood. He wrote to King Hiram of Tyre, 'I know how skilful your woodmen are, so send me cedar, cypress and juniper logs from Lebanon' (2 Chronicles 2:8). These are just a few of the trees used to build the temple.

Invite a timber merchant to come and show you the different kinds of timber used today and talk about their properties. If that is not possible, ask a woodyard for samples, and let the children feel the different textures and learn about their uses—and their costs—today.

THE SENSE OF SMELL

HOW DO I SMELL?

Tell the story of Jacob and Esau again, but this time have a selection of smells—the kinds one would find on a person.

> *You will need a selection of small covered pots containing baby powder, aftershave, lavender water, perfume, soap, toothpaste, shampoo, antiseptic lotion.*

Pass the items around one at a time. Can the children identify the smell? What kind of person does it remind them of? Where would they expect to smell it? Would the same person smell differently at different times?

HOW DO LEAVES SMELL?

If you cannot go to a park or wood, try this where you are.

> *You will need a selection of leaves from different trees, and a numbered card for each child.*

Display one set of leaves on a backing sheet. Write the name of each leaf on the sheet and number it. Then lay out a matching set on separate saucers, slightly crushed, and cover each of them with a light paper handkerchief. (Be sure the handkerchief isn't scented!)

Give each child a set of the numbers and ask them to sniff each covered saucer and match the leaf to the name and number on the displayed sheet. Can you find words to describe the smells?

OILS

Essential oils are expensive, but if you can mix small quantities of cypress, pine and cedar oils you may have some idea of how the temple smelled.

THE SENSE OF TASTE

THEY DO GROW ON TREES

Look around the shops and see how many fruits you can find that grow on trees. Some examples might be bananas, oranges, apples, dates. Discover how many come from Israel or nearby. Buy a few and chop them up to make a delicious fruit salad, sweetened with honey.

THAT RED STUFF

Read Genesis 25:27–34. Tradition says that Jacob's stew was made of red kidney beans. Let the children make a vegetable stew, using tinned red kidney beans. (Remember that kidney beans can be poisonous if not cooked sufficiently.)

> *You will need a tin of red kidney beans, aubergine, courgettes, onions, celery or any other vegetable of your choice, seasoning and flavourings such as sage and cumin.*

Prepare and chop the vegetables. Simmer them gently in a large saucepan for about 40 minutes, then add the kidney beans and cook for about 20 more minutes. When the stew is ready, let everyone enjoy their share with a chunk of crusty bread. You could add sage dumplings made with vegetarian suet at the same time as you add the kidney beans. (You'll find a recipe on the suet packet.)

THE ALMOND TREE

Read Numbers 17:1–11. The almond is the first tree to blossom in the spring.

Almonds are expensive, but here are some ideas for experiencing the taste.

- Blanch, peel and toast a few almonds.
- Use almond paste or marzipan to make miniature fruits, coloured with food colouring.
- Make some biscuits flavoured with almond essence, from the recipe below.

You will need:
- *110g each margarine and sugar, creamed together.*
- *1 egg, 3 or 4 drops almond essence, 1 rounded tablespoon honey, beaten in.*
- *225g self-raising flour, sifted and added to make firm dough.*
- *Flaked almonds (optional).*

Make the dough mixture into small balls on a greased baking tray, flatten slightly, add flaked almond if available, and bake at 180°C/Gas Mark 5 for 15 minutes.

STEP INTO PRAYER

PART OF GOD'S FAMILY

Read Psalm 105:1–11. Now read verses 7 and 8 again. Remember that Jesus told us we are part of his family, so these words are for us, too. Think about your part of the world. Does it still need God's commands? Think about 'for ever'. Do we still need his promises? Thank God for the freedom and plenty we enjoy. Ask him to show how can we help to make our part of the world a better place.

I HAVE CALLED YOU BY NAME

In Isaiah 43:1 God says of Israel, 'I have called you by name—you are mine.' Names are very important in the Bible. Abraham means 'ancestor of many nations', Isaac means 'he laughs' and Jacob means 'heel'. (Read Genesis 25:24–26 to find out more.) Do you know what your name means? Borrow a book from your library and find out. Now read those words from Isaiah again. God was speaking to you as well as Israel. Write your name on a card. Think about its meaning. Hold the card and say:

Thank you, God, that you have called
me… [your name].
Thank you that I'm yours.
Thank you that you are always with me,
and that my troubles will never
overwhelm me.
Amen.

WHAT KIND OF TREE ARE YOU?

Read Psalm 128. The vine and the olive tree both give fruit and live for many years. What else is special about them? Why would you want to be like them?

Paint a picture of the family around their table as shown in this psalm. Make vines and olive branches from crinkled paper, and paste them around and above the family.

Before the children take their pictures home, display them on a wall, and make this a focal point for prayers for families, both our own and others. Use this simple rhyme:

Lord, please bless my family,
Bless my friends, and God, bless me.
I know you'll always love me, so
I'll trust in you wherever I go.

Chapter 5

STEP INTO THE STORY
IN THE DESERT

LET MY PEOPLE GO

When Jacob's son, Joseph, became the governor of Egypt, all the family eventually joined him (after many adventures, which you can read about in the book of Genesis—chapters 37 to 50 are all about Joseph and his family). The Egyptians called the members of Joseph's family 'Hebrews', which means 'from far away'.

At first life was peaceful, but after 350 years the number of Hebrews living in Egypt had increased to hundreds of thousands and they were no longer welcome. Pharaoh, the king of Egypt, had a brilliant idea: all the Hebrews' baby boys must be drowned at birth! But one mother hid her baby in a floating basket. Pharaoh's daughter found him. She called him Moses and brought him up as a prince. Forty years later, Moses discovered that he

was a Hebrew, and knew that his people were being treated cruelly.

Moses left the palace and became a shepherd. One day on the mountains he saw flames coming from a bush, but the bush didn't burn up. Among the flames, there was an angel. From the bush, God told Moses that he must go to Pharaoh and ask him, 'Let my people go.'

Ten times Moses pleaded with Pharaoh. Ten times Pharaoh refused. So ten times God sent a plague to the Egyptians. All the water turned to blood. The land swarmed with frogs, gnats and flies. The livestock died. Everyone got horrible boils. There were hailstorms, locusts and total darkness. The last threat was the worst of all. All the first-born Egyptian sons would die. And Pharaoh still said 'No'.

God told the Hebrews to get ready to leave. They must kill a lamb, smear its blood on their doorposts, then cook and eat it. The blood would warn the angel of death to pass over their houses. Death touched every house of the Egyptians but passed over theirs.

The Hebrews set out on their journey, but Pharaoh's soldiers and chariots raced after them. Pharaoh needed his slaves! When they reached the Red Sea they were trapped. God told Moses to raise his hand. The sea parted, and the Israelites walked safely across. As the chariots hurtled after them, Moses lifted his hand again and the water rushed back, sweeping the Egyptians to their deaths.

Every year the Jewish people remember the bitterness and tears of slavery, the plagues, the blood on the doorposts, the final meal and the crossing of the Red Sea. They thank God for his great love and mercy, and celebrate their freedom.

STEP INTO THE FESTIVAL OF PASSOVER

THE PASSOVER

The Passover is the oldest and greatest festival of all. It is the spring 'pilgrimage' festival, the first of three. The *seder*, the Passover meal, was the occasion of Jesus' last supper with his disciples, and it is the pattern for the Christian communion service. We may be unable to follow the *seder* exactly or produce truly *kosher* food, but we can use many of the symbols to deepen our understanding. If you are unable to put the ideas into action, explain the symbols to the children.

The simplified *haggadah* (liturgy) on page 42 gives some idea of what it means for the Jewish people, and for us. You should recline on mats and cushions, with food on low tables, to show the Hebrews' new leisure and freedom.

You will need a candle and matches, small plastic glasses, red grape juice, a sprig of parsley for each person, one small bowl of salt water between 6–8 people and the following special foods:

- *Matzah: unleavened bread. If you cannot buy this, use plain water biscuits or dry crackers, or follow the recipe on page 45. You will need one cracker or half a piece of matzah per person.*
- *Haroset: a paste representing the mud used by the Hebrews to make bricks. See recipe on page 45.*
- *Maror: this means bitter herbs. Fresh horseradish is traditional, but you can substitute matchsticks of beetroot mixed with 1 teaspoon of horseradish sauce. A tablespoonful will suffice for eight people.*

To be *kosher* (fit and proper), the meal should include no raising agent, and if you are eating meat (for example, chicken drumsticks) you should not use dairy products of any kind. (You'll see why if you turn to page 58.) Suggestions for food could include fruit flapjacks, coconut pyramids, or meringue nests with fruit salad.

THE HAGGADAH

- When everyone is reclining comfortably, light a candle and say this blessing: 'Thank you, Lord, for your law, and this festive light.'
- Pour juice into each glass and say this blessing: 'Thank you, Lord, for bringing us out of slavery, and for the fruit of the vine.' Sip the juice.
- Wash hands. This is an important part of Jewish ritual. Yours can be a symbolic act of dipping hands into a bowl and wiping on a paper towel.
- Each person dips a piece of parsley into salted water. Say this blessing: 'Let us remember the hyssop dipped in blood.' Eat the parsley.
- The three youngest people present ask, 'Why is this night different to all other nights?' 'Why do we only eat unleavened bread?' 'Why do we eat bitter herbs?' The oldest person answers, 'To remember that we were all slaves in Egypt, and that if the Lord had not brought our fathers out, we would still be in bondage.'
- Say this blessing: 'Thank you, Lord, for our freedom.' Sip some juice.
- God brought these ten plagues on the Egyptians: blood, gnats, flies, pestilence, boils, hail, locusts, darkness, slaying of the first-born. (As each one is mentioned, dip a finger into the glass and flick the juice on to your plate.)
- Take a small piece of matzah, dip it into the haroset, and put in one piece of maror. Say, 'We remember the mud and bitterness of slavery.' Eat the matzah.
- Before the meal, say, 'Now let us celebrate the feast of life, and enjoy our food.' Eat.
- After the meal, say, 'Thank you, Lord, for the food you've provided, just as you promised Moses' (Deuteronomy 8:10).
- Read Matthew 26:26–28. Fill the glasses and give out small pieces of matzah. Say, 'Thank you, Lord, for giving us Jesus to be the bread of life.' Eat the matzah. Say, 'Thank you, Lord, for giving us Jesus to be the true vine.' Drink some juice.
- Say, 'The Passover is ended. May God grant that Jesus will return to Jerusalem and show himself to his people, Israel.' All respond, 'Next year in Jerusalem!'

THANKS TO MICHELE GUINNESS FOR PERMISSION TO USE IDEAS FROM HER BOOK, *A LITTLE KOSHER SEASONING*.

STEP INTO THE SENSES

THE SENSE OF SIGHT

NASTY CREATURES

Make headdresses to represent some of the plagues the Egyptians suffered, and have fun chasing one another.

You will need bands of strong card to go round the head (about 60cm long x 3cm wide), and photocopies of the templates of flies, frogs, gnats and locusts.

Let the children colour the pictures, cut them out, then glue or Sellotape them to the headbands.

For templates, see pages 171 and 172.

THE PILLAR OF CLOUD

Read Exodus 13:20–22. Close your eyes and try to imagine the scene. Now read Exodus 14:19–20. Do you see that there is something extra? Close your eyes again and paint the picture in your mind. Now open your eyes and paint the scene.

You will need a large piece of paper (at least A4) and paints in bright colours, gold and grey.

Paint the angel in the centre of the horizontal page, then paint the background with fiery colours on one side and grey on the other. When it is dry, make a pillar by overlapping the two edges and stapling them.

HIDE AND SEEK

Traditionally, a piece of matzah called the *afikomen* is wrapped in a napkin at the beginning of the *seder* and hidden. The children search for it at the end of the meal, with a prize for the finder. You could hide several napkins, with only one holding the *afikomen*. In modern Christian terms, this has become a symbol of the hidden Christ.

THE SENSE OF SOUND

DANCE AS MIRIAM DANCED

See how Miriam celebrated in Exodus 15:20–21. If you have no tambourines, use shakers, and play and dance to any of the following:

God is good (JP55)
Hallelu, hallelu (JP67)

LEARN HOW IT'S DONE

Invite the Salvation Army to send someone to teach you some of their timbrel (another name for tambourine) routines. They are very tricky—and effective. Listen to some of their music. They know how to celebrate!

BE CONFIDENT AND DETERMINED

This is a song to sing more thoughtfully, or perhaps as a march. God spoke these words three times to Joshua, Moses' successor, in Deuteronomy 31:6, 7 and 23. Sing the song 'Now be strong and very courageous' (JP172). Or you could sing the song, 'How did Moses cross the Red Sea?' (JP83).

THE SENSE OF TOUCH

CAMEL TRAIN

Make a few camels to help the Hebrews on their way.

You will need small plastic flower pots, stiff card, paste, clean old socks in grey or brown, and grey or brown knitting wool.

An adult can make a slit for the camel's head and a hole for its tail. Make the camel as illustrated, then cut patches of sock and paste them to cover its hump.

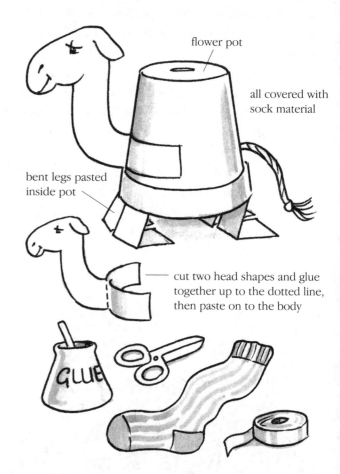

flower pot

all covered with sock material

bent legs pasted inside pot

cut two head shapes and glue together up to the dotted line, then paste on to the body

A BABY SAVED

Make a model of Moses hiding in his basket.

You will need clay, plasticine or playdough.

First make the basket, holding the lump of clay on the palm of one hand and hollowing it out with the opposite thumb. It should be about 7–8cm long. Now make a sausage shape to fit in the basket— that's Moses. You can mark his eyes and mouth and give him a little button nose. You can roll little squiggles for his hair. Now roll out a small piece of clay flat to make a 'blanket' to cover him.

THE SENSE OF SMELL

BITTER HERBS

Some herbs, like horseradish, can burn your tongue. They can also tickle your nose.

> *You will need a selection of flavourings in small dishes—horseradish, pepper, salt, chopped onion, garlic, mustard, a variety of vinegars and chutneys.*

Sniff the different flavourings, taking care not to inhale too deeply. Experiment to find which ones you would call 'bitter'.

HAROSET

Even the worst of jobs, like making bricks out of mud, can have a little sweetness. That's why haroset looks like mud, but tastes and smells sweet.

> *For 6–8 people, you will need 1 tablespoon chopped walnuts, 1 grated apple, 1 teaspoon cinnamon, 2 tablespoons grape juice, 1 tea-spoon honey.*

Pound these ingredients into a rough paste. Enjoy the smell, then eat the paste with wholemeal pitta bread.

THE SENSE OF TASTE

MATZAH

Try making your own substitute for Matzah.

> *You will need 225g plain flour (half white, half wholemeal), quarter tsp salt, 1 tablespoon vegetable oil, and enough water to make a stiff dough.*

Knead the ingredients well together, roll into a thin rectangle, cut into squares, place on a greased baking tray and prick with a fork. Cook at 180°C/Gas Mark 5 for about 20 minutes, until brown.

NEW LIFE

> *You will need hard-boiled eggs, mayonnaise, crackers.*

Eggs were offered in the temple at Passover as a sign of new life. The Passover *seder* should start with egg, but you can use them any time. Slice some hard-boiled eggs, spread mayonnaise on small crackers, place a slice of egg on top, and add a sprig of parsley. Eat and enjoy. Happy new life!

RED SEA SALAD

> *You will need shredded lettuce, fingers of celery, slices of cucumber, beetroot and orange, honey and orange juice.*

Spread the lettuce at the bottom of a dish to represent the sea. Heap the celery, cucumber, beetroot and orange to represent Pharaoh's broken chariots, and dribble a little orange and honey over the top to season. Share and enjoy.

STEP INTO PRAYER

GOD'S PROTECTION

Numbers 19:18 tells the people of Israel how to purify a tent where someone has died: it must be sprinkled with a sprig of fragrant hyssop dipped in water. On their final night in Egypt, God told the Israelites to mark their doorposts with hyssop dipped in lamb's blood.

Talk about things we have to protect us today, such as cleaning materials, medicines and vaccinations. Draw a big door on a piece of paper. Mark the doorframe with red paint to represent blood, and write a 'thank you' on the other side for all the things that protect us.

Use a sprig of rosemary in place of hyssop and sprinkle the door and windows of your room with water, asking God to protect you from thinking bad thoughts.

SENT BY THE LORD

Read Exodus 3:9–10. Why didn't God speak to Pharaoh himself? We know that God can do anything. But he loves to be with people and work with them. Now read Exodus 4:10–11. Moses didn't want to be a prophet. He didn't want to go to the king. But God persuaded him, and got his brother to help!

Think about things we can do on our own but prefer to do with someone else. It might be a film, a meal or shopping. It might be something worrying—a visit to the dentist or hospital. Share your thoughts, then thank God for giving you the right person to be with you when you need them.

Say 'God, I know I can… on my own, but thank you for letting… go with me.'

PRAISE GOD

Read Psalm 66:5–9 and 20 very slowly and prayerfully. Can we think of times when God 'did not reject our prayers'?

Chapter 6

STEP INTO THE STORY OF GOD'S RULES

RULES FOR THE FAMILY

EXODUS 20—32

The Israelites set off on their journey to the promised land. Moses was their leader for 40 years, but God himself led them, hidden in a pillar of cloud by day and of fire by night.

Every family needs rules, and this family needed them badly. They were always arguing, so Moses appointed some judges to help him.

God told the people, 'If you will obey me and keep my covenant, you will be my own people.' God arranged to meet Moses on Mount Sinai, where he gave him these rules:

- Do not worship any God but me.
- Do not make images and worship them.
- Do not use my name wrongly.
- Keep the Sabbath day holy. That was the day I rested.
- Respect your father and mother.
- Do not commit murder.
- Do not take another person's husband or wife.
- Do not steal.
- Do not accuse anyone falsely.
- Do not desire what another person owns.

God engraved these commandments on stone tablets. Moses made a sacred box and tent for them. When he returned 40 days later, he found the people dancing round a golden calf. They had already broken the first two commandments!

Moses was horrified. He flung the tablets to the ground, shattering them. God sent a plague as punishment, but Moses begged him not to abandon them. Then Moses wrote the commandments on new tablets. The Israelites had to learn that God meant business.

God travelled with his people in the pillar of cloud. It covered the tent when he wanted them to rest, and led the way when it was time to move on.

God gave many other rules about how the people of Israel should live and worship him, but these ten commandments are the ones we still follow today. You'll see that God has a good reason for every one of them.

Just before he died, Jesus said, 'And now I give you a new commandment: love one another. As I have loved you, so you must love one another. If you love one another, then everyone will know that you are my disciples' (John 13:34–35).

STEP INTO THE FESTIVAL OF SHAVUOT

SHAVUOT

Shavuot is the Feast of the Harvest, the second pilgrimage festival of the year. It is held 50 days (seven weeks) after Passover. *Shavuot* means 'seven weeks'. We now know it as Pentecost. It celebrates Moses receiving God's teaching on Mount Sinai. On that day, homes and synagogues are decked with flowers as a reminder of the flowers that bloomed on the mountain. It is also the occasion for offering the first fruits to God.

Tradition says that Moses was away so long that all the milk turned to cheese, hence the tradition of eating dairy produce. No meat is eaten, but treats such as cheesecakes and fried pancakes (blintzes) are allowed.

DOS AND DON'TS

When Moses had finished giving God's teachings to the people, he said, 'Make sure you obey all these commands that I have given you today. Repeat them to your children, so that they may faithfully obey all God's teachings. These teachings are not empty words; they are your very life' (Deuteronomy 32:45–47). Imagine being the first person ever to have a Bible!

Look at the ten commandments. Eight of them begin with 'Do not…'. Can you rewrite them so that they mean the same but start without 'Do not'? For instance, the first one could be 'Worship God with all your heart.' You could work in pairs, then compare notes.

SEVEN THINGS

Read Proverbs 6:16–19. Think about the seven things the Lord cannot stand. Now go through the ten commandments and check whether these seven rules make sense. Do you think we would still need the commandments if everyone kept those seven rules?

RUTH'S STORY

The story of Ruth was a traditional reading for *Shavuot*. That is because the festival coincides with the barley harvest, when an important part of Ruth's story took place. It tells how a Moabite woman, because of her great love and loyalty, became part of God's family—and an ancestor of Jesus. You can read the story of Ruth in the book named after her (it comes after Judges and before 1 Samuel in the Bible), or read about her in a children's Bible or book of Bible stories.

STEP INTO THE SENSES

THE SENSE OF SIGHT

THANKSGIVING FLAGS

Make your own flags of thanksgiving.

For each flag, you will need a pole or stick about 30cm long (available in garden shops), pieces of coloured A5 paper, crayons or marker pens, and Sellotape.

Draw or paint one of the things we might celebrate during *Shavuot*, such as fruits and flowers and God's word, on each flag. Try to have as many different ones as possible. Fasten the picture to your pole with Sellotape.

FIRST FRUITS

Read Deuteronomy 26:1–11. At *Shavuot* even the king had to carry his basket of fruits to the priests in person.

Play a 'first fruits' game, perhaps in groups of two or three.

You will need a tray with a display of wheat, barley, grapes, olives, pomegranates, dates and figs, plus seven sheets of paper with an anagram of one of these fruits and grains written on each sheet.

Photocopy the sheets of paper showing the seven words jumbled up, so that each group has a set of all seven words. Look at what's on the tray, then try to find the word on the sheet. Finally write it correctly. The first group to complete the game gets a small prize of fruit.

THE BURNING BUSH

Read Exodus 3:1–6. Paint a picture of the bush Moses saw, but use green paper to cut or tear out leaves, and red, yellow and orange to make flames. Stick them on so that they look real. Don't forget the angel.

You will need a large sheet of paper, paints, crepe paper in green, red, yellow and orange, and paste.

THE SENSE OF SOUND

JUBILATE

The first fruits were carried with much rejoicing, and flutes were played. Now is the time for people to show what they can do, if not in flute-playing, perhaps with a recorder. If they can play the tune of 'Jubilate' (JP145), you could sing and dance to this.

If you haven't done an Israeli circle dance, try now. Stand in a circle, hands on your neighbour's shoulder. Move right foot in front of left, move left foot to left, right foot behind left, left foot to left, repeat.

SPIRIT OF THE LIVING GOD

When the world was created, the Spirit of God was moving. Sometimes we think of a wind or breath, but the Spirit of God can also be a fire. The glory of the Lord is called *Shekinah* in Hebrew.

Jesus' followers were filled with the Holy Spirit at Pentecost, after his resurrection. They heard a strong wind blowing and saw tongues of fire (Acts 2:1–2).

Sing the song 'Spirit of the living God' (JP222). Alternatively, sing the song 'All over the world' (JP5).

THE SENSE OF TOUCH

THE FEEL OF WHEAT

Wheat was offered at the festival of *Shavuot*.

You will need wheat grain, flour, cereals, semolina, couscous and pasta.

Feel the difference between grains of wheat and wheat flour. Find out how the wheat is processed to make flour. Enjoy a dish of wheat cereal with milk, and perhaps sugar or honey.

A	B	C	D	E
F	G	H	I	J
K	L	M	N	O
P	Q	R	S	T
U	V	W	X	Y
Z	and	for	of	the

FINGER READING

Louis Braille, a blind Frenchman, invented a way for blind people to read with their fingers. The system is called 'Braille'. You can write a message in Braille that a blind person can read.

You will need a piece of corrugated card, a sheet of graph paper and something to punch holes with. (This could be a fine knitting needle or nail.)

Fix the paper on to the corrugated card with Blu-tack. The message 'Happy Pentecost' is illustrated below. Copy it on to your paper. The message is written backwards, from right to left. The reader will turn the paper over and read from left to right.

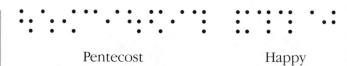

Pentecost   Happy

Using the Braille alphabet at the top of this column, try to write your name too. Can you work out how to write other messages? Remember to leave a space between words.

Turn the paper over to read your messages. Can you feel the points with your fingertips?

Ask your local Association for the Blind if there's anyone who would like to receive a card from you.

THE SENSE OF SMELL

SMELL SWEET

When they were celebrating in the synagogues, Jewish girls sometimes wore floral headbands. Girls can make their own headband; boys can make a floral buttonhole instead.

> *For each headband, you will need three strands of raffia to fit round your head, and some sweet-smelling flowers with short stalks. For a buttonhole, use flowers, raffia and a safety-pin.*

Make a plaited headband. Hold the three strands of raffia with a paperclip, plait them, then knot all the ends together. Slot flowers through the raffia, and hold them in place with Sellotape at the back.

For a buttonhole, take a few flowers and bind their stems with raffia. Fix to your shirt with a safety-pin.

WHAT'S THAT CHEESE?

Buy a selection of the stronger-smelling cheeses. Arrange them on a plate or tray. Can the children name any of them? If not, try to find words that describe what they can smell. Lastly, taste small samples.

THE SENSE OF TASTE

WHEAT AND CHEESE

Loaves of fresh bread were offered in the temple at *Shavuot.*

> *For a simple feast, you will need some small fluffy bread buns, jam or honey, and cream cheese or other cheese.*

Make your own feast, celebrating the wheat, the fruits and the dairy produce.

TZATZIKI

Read Numbers 11:4–6. When the people became fed up with wandering in the desert, they longed for the things they'd once enjoyed in Egypt. Close your eyes and imagine you've just stepped off your camel in Egypt. Here's a way to enjoy those cool cucumbers!

You will need half a cucumber, small pot of yoghurt, mint, clove of garlic.

Peel and slice the cucumber and press the slices to remove excess moisture. Cut into strips. Cut the mint with blunt scissors. Press the garlic. Mix all together with a little salt and pepper, and enjoy with pitta bread.

CHEESE BLINTZES

These are a great favourite for *Shavuot*.

For pancake batter, you will need 120g flour, 220ml milk, 2 eggs, pinch of salt, 2 tbsp melted butter.

Mix the ingredients well together until completely smooth. The younger children can do this. Older children or adults can then cook the pancakes by pouring the mixture on to a hot frying pan, first greasing the pan with oil.

For filling, use 450g cottage or cream cheese and let the children choose their own flavouring—add cinnamon or grated lemon rind with sugar. Put a spoonful of the mixture in each pancake and roll it. The finished pancake should be fried, but instead you can butter the top and crisp it in a hot oven or under a grill for a few minutes.

STEP INTO PRAYER

WAVE THOSE FLAGS

If you made thanksgiving flags, use them now. Think about the ten commandments and how they keep us safe. Think about Moses. Think about those who translated and printed our Bibles. Think about being able to read and understand.

March with your flags, singing and dancing.

YOUR OFFERING

Make a display of the things offered in the 'First fruits' activity on page 49. If you cannot use fresh fruit, let the children cut pictures from magazines and paste them on to a paper plate.

You will need paper plates, lots of magazines with fruit pictures, paste, scissors.

Use your display as a focal point for a prayer of thanksgiving. Talk about all the first fruits you have experienced—for example, the first book you read. The first time you read a book, write a letter, swim, ride a bike, or enjoy another new experience, thank God for it.

SOMEONE'S BROUGHT A LOAF OF BREAD

Sing this song together (JP220).

You will need a loaf of bread and a jar of jam, plus other items of your choice.

As you sing, march or dance until all the things are on a central table. For the final verse, if possible join hands and skip in a circle around the table.

A NEW COMMANDMENT

Remember the new commandment that Jesus gave us? On a piece of card, draw an outline of the two tablets that Moses inscribed with the ten commandments. Draw a picture of yourself on one tablet, and people you love on the other. Use the picture to thank God for Jesus and the people you love. Write 'Love one another' over the top and give it to someone special.

Chapter 7

STEP INTO THE STORY OF A KINGDOM

WE WANT A KING!

With Moses as their leader, Israel became a nation. Now they wanted to be like other nations. 'We want a king!' they cried.

First they asked Gideon, 'Be our ruler', but Gideon said, 'I will not be your ruler, nor will my son. The Lord will be your ruler.' His son, Abimelech, had other ideas. He killed his 70 brothers and had himself made king—but not for long.

The people cried out once more, 'We want a king!' Their leader, Samuel, was old and wise. God warned that if they had a king, they would have to work like slaves to pay for all his splendour. But they insisted, 'We want a king!' Sadly, God told Samuel, 'Give them a king', and Saul was chosen.

Saul reigned for 40 years, but power drove him mad. He was jealous of David, the boy whom God had chosen to take his place. Saul and his son, Jonathan—David's dear friend—were both killed in battle.

David was a shepherd in Bethlehem, and he was his father's youngest son. His strength was amazing. He killed the giant Goliath with one shot from his sling. He was a fine musician, and we still sing the songs he wrote. He made Jerusalem a great city. He built a holy place for the tablets of the law. David did some foolish, wicked things, but he loved God, and was truly sorry, so God forgave him. David was special because he was Jesus' ancestor.

David's son, Solomon, built the great temple in Jerusalem. But the palaces he built for his 700 wives were four times bigger! God's warning came true: the people had to pay for it all. Once more they forgot about God. The kingdom was divided, with Israel in the north and Judah in the south. There were many other kings, some good, some bad, but both Israel and Judah were conquered at last.

Zedekiah, the last king of Judah, came to a terrible end. King Nebuchadnezzar of Babylon killed his two sons, blinded him, and dragged him off in chains. The people were taken captive for 70 years.

Then God sent Jesus to show the world what a king should be. His stories about the kingdom of God are mind-boggling—the kingdom is here already, and we belong to it.

STEP INTO THE FESTIVAL OF BAR MITZVAH

THE BOOKS OF KINGS

Israel had been blessed with good leaders like Moses, Joshua and Samuel, but they insisted on a king. God's choice of a king was unexpected. He knows the hearts of human beings and sees what no one else sees.

Many of the stories about Saul, David, Solomon and other kings can be found in colourful books of Bible stories, or children's Bibles. Encourage the children to read and dramatize them.

OUR BODIES

Read Deuteronomy 6:6–9. The Israelite men were told to write out the words of the prayer *Shema Yisrael* and wear them on their head and arm. They made leather boxes called *t'fillin*, put the parchments inside them, and tied them to their heads and arms with long strips of leather. Many still do this today at prayer time.

The men also wear a *tallit* (prayer shawl) with a *tzitzit* (tassel) on each corner. (Ideas for making tassels are given on page 57.)

Women always cover their heads. Today some Jewish women wear a wig to make sure their own head is never seen. If their hair can be seen, it isn't real!

What things do we wear today that tell people what we believe?

KOSHER FOOD

Read about kosher food on page 58. What rules for food do we have which are hard to explain?

BAR MITZVAH

When Jesus was a child, boys started to study the Hebrew Bible when they were about six. Six years later they spent a year learning parts of it by heart, and at the age of thirteen became adult members of the synagogue. Jewish boys do the same today, and go through an important ceremony called *bar mitzvah*. That means 'son of the law'. Today some girls have the same ceremony when they are twelve. Theirs is called *bat mitzvah*, 'daughter of the law'.

STEP INTO THE SENSES

THE SENSE OF SIGHT

THE STAR OF DAVID

The Star of David is one of the national symbols of Israel.

To make a star, you will need some stiff card and paper of silver and gold.

Cut six narrow pieces of card (all the same length), then glue them at the corners to make triangles. Now put the two triangles together as shown and fix with staples. Cover with silver or gold paper. Use fine thread to hang the star in your room, or make several for a mobile.

A KINGLY T-SHIRT

Paint your own T-shirt.

You will need a clean, ironed T-shirt, soft pencil, fabric paints or permanent marker pens in bright colours, including gold or silver.

Make sure your T-shirt is clean and ironed. Put a piece of thick card and plastic sheeting between the front and back to prevent the colours seeping through. Hold it steady with large paperclips.

Practise drawing a very simple design before you start. Some ideas are given below. Choose your own size. Draw it on the shirt with a soft pencil.

(This will wash out later.) When you are sure it is right, draw the lines very carefully with a dark marker pen. Then fill in the shape with gold pen or yellow fabric paint.

You could also use this method to decorate pillowcases or handkerchiefs.

I WILL SING AS DAVID SANG

Read about King David dancing in 2 Samuel 6:1–5 and 16.

Sing the song 'When the Spirit of the Lord…' (SF 598).

When you are sure of the words, have a traditional circle dance. Instructions can be found under 'Jubilate' on page 50.

KINGS AND SHEPHERDS

You will need a taped recording of 'Lift up your heads' from Handel's Messiah.

Read Psalm 23:1. Now read Psalm 24:7–8. Compare the two. God knows that sometimes we need a gentle helper, sometimes a mighty warrior.

Sing the first verse of the hymn 'The Lord's my shepherd' (JP243). Next, play the tape from *Messiah*. (You may want to fade out after the main theme.) Encourage a sing-along!

THE SENSE OF TOUCH

SHEMA

'Israel, remember this! The Lord—and the Lord alone—is our God.' This special prayer, the *Shema*, is found in Deuteronomy 6:4. Now read verses 5–9.

The *Shema* is written on a scroll and put in a special box called a *mezuzah*. You can make one and fix it inside your front door, or perhaps your own bedroom.

To make a mezuzah, *you will need an empty toothpaste box or similar small packet, covered with coloured paper and decorated.*

You could paste a cut-out Star of David or *menorah* (seven-branched candlestick) on to your *mezuzah*.

Write the words of the *Shema* as neatly as you can on a piece of quality paper. Roll the paper up as a scroll and put it inside the *mezuzah*, which you can attach to your doorpost with Blu-tack.

MAKE YOUR OWN TZITZIT

Tzitzit is the Hebrew word for 'tassel'. Jewish people have a tassel on each corner of their prayer shawls, but you can make some to decorate scarves or winter caps. A strand of blue represents holiness.

You will need knitting wool (ideally white plus a short length of blue), two squares of stiff card 8cm wide, and a blunt darning needle.

Put the squares of card together. Wind the wool around them, loosely, 20–25 times. Break off the wool and add a strand of blue. Take another short piece and loop it through the wool at what will be the top. Tie the strands together firmly. Now cut the loop between the cards at the bottom. Finally, remove the card and wind a length of wool a few times near the top of the loop, as illustrated.

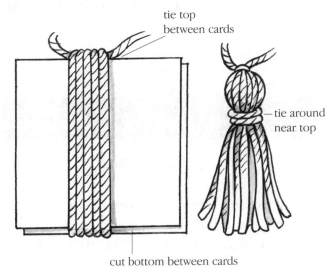

tie top between cards

tie around near top

cut bottom between cards

You could stitch the tassel on a winter cap, or make more and stitch them on to scarves. Make a smaller one and attach it to a piece of card as a bookmark.

THE SENSE OF SMELL

THE COST OF FRAGRANCE

In 1 Samuel 8:13, Samuel warned that if the people had a king, their daughters would have 'to make perfumes for him'—instead of all the helpful things a daughter would do at home.

Go around the shops with a notebook and check the price of the most expensive perfume you can find. Ask women friends to let you have a squirt of their favourite one. Look at the men's aftershaves, too. Are they really worth the money? What else could you spend the money on?

WASH YOUR HANDS

To the Jewish people, the washing of hands before touching food is very important. It is part of the ritual of the Passover *seder*.

Find a fragrant soap that has something regal about it, and take turns to wash hands before enjoying one of the following foods. Use a soft brush for fingernails and a fresh towel. Enjoy the before-and-after effect.

THE SENSE OF TASTE

KOSHER FOOD

Kosher means 'fit, proper'. Some of the rules for kosher food seem strange to us. Jewish people never eat meat and milk together. Meat and dairy products are cooked in separate utensils. The utensils are then washed in separate sinks. The reason for this can be found in Exodus 23:19. Their neighbours, the Canaanites, worshipped foreign gods. In one of their rituals they would boil a baby goat in its mother's milk. The Israelites thought this was cruel. They did not want to copy them, even by mistake. The Jews still follow this rule today. That means no cheeseburgers! Look at the rules in Leviticus 11. How would they affect you?

FALAFELS

Enjoy one of modern Israel's favourite foods.

> You will need a tin of chickpeas (400g), a small chopped onion, salt and pepper, 1 teaspoon cumin, and a clove of garlic (crushed).

Drain the chickpeas, pound them to a pulp and mix with the other ingredients. Form into small cakes or balls and bake on a greased tray at 180°C/Gas Mark 5 for about twelve minutes. Drop a few into half a pitta bread with some shredded lettuce, and enjoy.

FIG TRUFFLES

In Isaiah 38:21 we read how the prophet Isaiah used fig paste to heal King Hezekiah's boil. In Jeremiah 24:1–8 we read of another king of Judah being compared to a bad fig. Figs were a common and valued food in Old Testament times. Today they are expensive, but you could use a small amount in these delicious truffles, which would make lovely gifts.

> You will need 85g each sultanas and figs, 55g each raisins, prunes, crushed biscuits, 30g dried coconut, l tsp apricot jam, 1 tbsp orange juice.

Cut the fruit into small pieces with scissors, and mix all well together, adding the juice gradually to make a stiff paste. Form the mixture into about 40 balls, rolling them in more dried coconut, and stand the balls in paper cases.

Alternatively, buy some fig biscuits and enjoy them together.

STEP INTO PRAYER

PRAY FOR LEADERS

In Psalm 89 the psalmist says that God made his servant, David, king and calls him 'the greatest of all kings' (vv. 20–21, 27).

Pray for the leaders of our country, that they may be not only great, but servants who listen to the Lord and ask for his guidance. The children may know the names of some of our leaders, either in government or locally. Let them pray for them by name. What blessings do we want them to have? What would we like them to do for us?

PRAY FOR OURSELVES

Psalm 89 says that God's strength will always be with King David and God's power will make him strong. David says of God, 'You are my father and my God, you are my protector and saviour' (vv. 21, 26).

We can't all be 'the greatest of all kings', but we can be like David in other ways. How many ways can you think of? For example, David was God's servant.

Make a list of all the things we have in common with David.

Pray through the list, asking that each one of us may share David's good qualities.

PRAY FOR ANYTHING!

The Jewish people ask God to bless anything in their lives—their homes and families, their work, or anything that is part of them. God's quite happy to bless anything—like a new pair of shoes or a new tooth. He knows every part of you, including every hair on your head, so don't be afraid to ask for his blessing.

Chapter 8

STEP INTO THE STORY
OF A PROMISE

YOU HAVE BEEN WARNED!

'If you don't… clean your teeth/fasten your seatbelt…'. 'If you… eat too many sweets/play with fire…'. Yes, warnings can be annoying, but they're usually a sign that someone cares about us.

God's warnings always came with a promise. The people had ignored him, and they would be punished and Jerusalem would be destroyed. But he would always love them and welcome them back.

Sometimes God speaks in person. Sometimes he sends angels. But for 300 years he sent prophets, ordinary human messengers, to speak for him. Let's look at some of the people God used.

About 870 years before Jesus was born, Ahab was king of Israel. The Bible says, 'Ahab did more things to disobey the Lord than any king before him' (1 Kings 16:30, CEV). Ahab had built a temple for Baal in Samaria, so Elijah warned him that there would be no rain for three years. Elijah had an amazing contest with 400 of Baal's prophets to show who was really God. Guess who won!

When Elijah died, his young helper, Elisha, carried on his work. They were good, kind men. The Bible says that Elijah's body was carried up to heaven, and Jews believe that he will return one day. (But we know that he talked to Jesus—Matthew says so in chapter 17 of his Gospel!)

A hundred years later, Israel and Judah were at war. God sent Amos, a farmhand, to tell how the poor and weak were being badly treated. He sent Hosea to show how much he loved his people. He told Hosea to marry an unfaithful wife and keep on loving her. The people could see how painful this was for Hosea—and for God.

Isaiah warned the people that they would be carried away to Babylon. But we'll leave Isaiah's greatest news until the last story. Jeremiah is the saddest prophet of all, but he also gave God's wonderful promise: 'I will forgive their sins and I will no longer remember their wrongs' (Jeremiah 31:34).

There were more prophets. God really made sure that the people heard his warnings. Most of the time they didn't listen. They had to suffer for many years before all the great promises were fulfilled.

STEP INTO THE FESTIVAL OF HANUKKAH

THE MIRACLE OF THE OIL

There's a story from the book of 2 Maccabees (which is in the part of the Old Testament known as the Apocrypha, found in some Bibles between the Old and New Testaments). From the story comes a legend that the Jewish people still celebrate. The Syrians had conquered Israel. They ordered the Israelites to ignore all the laws God had given them. They took over the temple in Jerusalem, put up a statue of a pagan god, and sacrificed pigs on the altar.

One family rebelled. They were nicknamed 'Maccabees', which means 'hammer-like'. After many battles they recaptured the defiled temple. It was in a ruinous, disgusting state. Everything had to be cleaned out and made new. There was enough purified oil left to light the *Menorah* (the sacred lamp) for only one day. But it stayed alight for eight days, until more oil was found.

To Noah, God gave the sign of the rainbow. To the Jews who cleaned and rededicated the temple, he gave this other sign of fresh hope. It is celebrated each year at *Hanukkah*, the Jewish Festival of Lights. It's a time of great rejoicing and thanksgiving, with fun and feasting. People light a special lamp with eight candles, and a centre one called 'the Servant', to remember those eight days. They light lamps outside and inside their homes. They give gifts. They eat foods made with oil. *Hanukkah* can help us to celebrate God's hands-on approach to life.

WHO'S YOUR WATCHMAN?

In Ezekiel 33:1–9 God appoints the prophet Ezekiel as a watchman. There used to be a programme on TV called *Dad's Army*, set during the Second World War. It was all about the men who stayed at home to watch out for the enemy. The programme was funny, but also true. Can you think of any other people who are watchmen for us? Or are you a watchman in some way? Talk about what happens when a watchman doesn't do his job.

Make up a play, with the watchman falling asleep, reading a book or writing a letter. The rest of you, the enemy, creep up on him or her. How much noise do you have to make before he raises the alarm?

STEP INTO THE SENSES

THE SENSE OF SIGHT

HANUKKIAH

'Hanukkiah' is the name of the special lamp with nine candles.

You will need modelling clay or playdough, nine small candles and candleholders, a strip of card 27cm long and 4cm wide.

Make ten small balls of clay, each one large enough to stick a candle in. Press the balls firmly on to a cardboard base, with four on each side, and two pressed together at the centre. Use coloured playdough, or paint the clay when it is dry. The centre candle is lit first, then used to light the others.

IS IT STRAIGHT?

In Amos 7:7–9 the prophet has a vision about a plumb-line. Look around your room. Are the walls straight? Are you sure? Make your own plumb-line.

You will need 2–3 metres of cord with something small but heavy tied to the bottom.

Ask an adult to help. Someone will need to climb on a stepladder near the corner of the room and use the plumb-line to check how straight the wall is. Now check the door frame.

Warning: you must first check that stepladders or chairs don't wobble, and have someone to hold them steady.

Some things aren't as straight as they look. Does that apply to people, too?

JEREMIAH'S CLAY

In Jeremiah 18:1–6, God uses a potter working at his wheel to show the prophet Jeremiah how to help the people to see that God wants them to change their evil ways. God never gets tired of trying to bring us back to him when we go wrong.

You will need a lump of clay or playdough for each person.

Can you make a perfect cup or bowl? Try, and whenever you're not satisfied, pull it apart and try again.

AS SURE AS THE SUNRISE

Make a gift card. In Lamentations 3:22–23 we read the words, 'The Lord's unfailing love and mercy still continue; fresh as the morning, as sure as the sunrise.'

Learn these words by heart. Write them inside the card, and on the outside draw a picture of the sun rising over the horizon. (The words could be photocopied for younger children.) Give the card to someone who needs cheering up.

THE SENSE OF SOUND

DID YOU HEAR ME?

In Nehemiah 9:30–31, the prophet Nehemiah says to God, 'Year after year you patiently warned them. You inspired your prophets to speak, but your people were deaf.'

Tell half of the children to block their ears. (No cheating!) Tell the others to close their eyes. Now tell them all quietly but clearly, 'You're in great danger. Leviathan's coming to gobble up anyone he finds in the wrong place. So when I say "Go", if you're wearing short socks, move to the left. If they're long, move to the right.' (You can make your own choice of instruction.)

If any 'deaf' children move, check their socks. If they're in the wrong place, make them sit down again.

Talk about how important it is to hear warnings.

A SOFT WHISPER

In 1 Kings 19:9–13, we read how discouraged Elijah was, and who would blame him? But God made sure Elijah would listen to him.

Find the story in your Bible. Start reading verse 11 aloud from 'Then the Lord…'

- After 'the rocks', boys call out, 'Elijah, Elijah, Elijah'.
- After 'earthquake', everybody shouts, 'Elijah, wake up!'
- After 'fire', the girls call (not so loudly), 'Listen, Elijah, listen, Elijah'.
- Speak the rest quietly, and when you reach 'Elijah, what are you doing here?' whisper.

SING THESE SONGS

Here are two songs that you could sing.

Give me oil in my lamp (JP 50)
This little light of mine (JP258)

THE SENSE OF TOUCH

EZEKIEL'S DRY BONES

The prophet Ezekiel's name means 'God strengthens'. He was deported to Babylon when Jerusalem fell to the Babylonians in 586BC.

In Ezekiel 37:1–14, we read about a vision Ezekiel had of a valley of dry bones. Let's put some life on to those bones!

You will need lengths of wire or pipe cleaners from an art or craft shop (about 15cm in length), pieces of newspaper, thick wallpaper paste, brushes, paint.

Twist the pieces of wire to make skeletons, bending the ends to make feet, hands and a head. Decide how you want them to stand or sit. Cover them with layers of glued paper, scrunching up bigger pieces to make the head, hands, feet and thicker parts of the body. Finish with a smooth layer, and allow to dry near a radiator or in the sunshine. When the model is dry, paint it flesh-coloured, and clothe it with scraps of paper or cloth.

Mix all the ingredients together. Drop spoonfuls of the mixture on to a greased, shallow baking pan. Bake for about 20 minutes at 170°C/Gas Mark 5, turning over halfway through the cooking time. (This is safer than the traditional method of frying in hot fat, although an older child or adult could do that.)

GOD CALLS ISAIAH

In Isaiah 6:1–8, we read how God touched Isaiah's mouth to clear away any impurities. Write your own drama to show how God called Isaiah to be a prophet, using a piece of crinkled shiny red paper for the burning coal.

THE SENSE OF SMELL

POTATO LATKES

There's nothing like the smell of fried onions! These potato and onion cakes smell good and taste wonderful.

> You will need 3 potatoes (grated and squeezed in a cloth to remove surplus moisture), 1 large onion (grated), 1 egg, quarter of a cup of flour, pinch of salt.

SWEET-SMELLING CANDLES

Instead of the *hanukkiah* made from clay, use floating candles.

> You will need a large glass bowl filled with water and nine floating candles, one of a different colour.

Inexpensive tea-lights in a metal case will float. A fancy bowl would look good, but a Pyrex casserole will do. If you have no scented candles, drop a few drops of fragrant bath oil in the water.

Warning: when lighting candles, never lean across those that are already lit.

INCENSE

In Exodus 30:34–38, we read that God wanted his holy place to have a fragrant smell. Another name for frankincense is olibanum, which means 'oil of Lebanon'. It is used in the mixture known as incense. Light a stick of incense, close your eyes and let your minds go back to that time and place.

THE SENSE OF TASTE

ANYONE FOR CHIPS?

Have a bring-and-share feast where you can all bring something like a packet of crisps or some doughnuts. Perhaps you could cook some oven chips.

OLIVE OIL

Look at the selection of oils on your supermarket shelves. How many different kinds can you find? Olive oil is still special today. If possible, try one or two varieties. Use it as a dip for lettuce and raw vegetables cut into strips. Try mixing it with vinegar to make a salad dressing. Enjoy a few olives with it.

POPCORN (FOR OLDER CHILDREN)

You will need a packet of popping corn, some vegetable oil and a heavy pan.

Heat two or three tablespoons of vegetable oil in the pan, pour some of the corn into it and put the lid on firmly. Shake from time to time. Cook at moderate heat until the popping ceases. Always wait a few moments to make sure it has finished. Pour out and sprinkle with salt.

Warning: do not let younger children handle the hot, heavy pan.

STEP INTO PRAYER

OH NO, YOU'RE NOT

Jeremiah told God, 'I don't know how to speak; I am too young.' When God asked Moses to speak for him, Moses said, 'I can't speak properly.' When he asked Jonah to go for him, Jonah said, 'I don't want to help those people.' When God calls you to do something for him, what will you say? Say this rhyme together:

Thank you, God, that I'm not too small
(crouch down)
That I'm not too large
(hands held out wide)
And I'm not too tall (reach up on tiptoe)
Thank you, God, that you made me ME
(pat chest)
And that I'm just the way (hands out)
You want me to be (point upwards)
Thank you for giving me all that I need
(hands out)
So that when you call me
(hands to mouth)
I'll go—agreed! (thumbs up)

JOEL'S VISION

In Joel 2:28–29, the prophet Joel is given this message from God: 'I will pour out my Spirit on everyone. Your sons and daughters will dream dreams.'

What dreams do you have for the future—not just for yourself, but for the world? Peace? No more hunger? Can you paint a picture of a vision that you have? Make this picture your prayer.

Pray, 'Dear God, please send your Holy Spirit to me, and let me share your visions for the future. Amen.'

EZEKIEL'S TREE

In Ezekiel 17:22–23, we read about a tall cedar tree in which every kind of bird will find shelter. Let's make Ezekiel's tree full of birds.

You will need a large piece of lining paper with a tree roughly painted on it, and paste.

Let each child cut out a bird shape and write their name on it. Thank God for his love for every individual, whoever we are. As they paste their bird on the tree, say a prayer of thanks. You could also add leaves to the tree and pray for others.

EZEKIEL'S TREE

Chapter 9

STEP INTO THE STORY OF GOD'S JUDGMENT

BY THE RIVERS OF BABYLON

'By the rivers of Babylon we sat down; there we wept when we remembered Zion. Those who captured us told us to… "Sing us a song about Zion." How can we sing a song to the Lord in a foreign land?'

The Hebrews were slaves in Babylon for 70 years. These words from Psalm 137 describe their great sadness. (Zion is another name for Jerusalem.)

God and the prophets had warned them. Their great leaders, Moses and Joshua, had warned them, but they hadn't listened.

First the Assyrians captured Israel in the north, and destroyed its capital, Samaria. A hundred years later the Babylonians attacked Judah in the south and destroyed Jerusalem. As slaves in Babylon, the people of Israel were called 'Jews', from the name 'Judah'.

Nebuchadnezzar, the wicked king of Babylon, trained some of the brightest young slaves to serve him. (Read Daniel 3 to find out what happened to Daniel's friends when they refused to worship a statue of the king.) When Daniel was an old man… but you can read that story in Daniel 6. Let us just say that Daniel stayed faithful to God all his life.

You can read all about these sad times in Lamentations. The Jewish people had no temple, but they remembered to pray. At the end of this book they cry, 'But you, O Lord, are king for ever, and will rule to the end of time' (Lamentations 5:19).

God used a strange mixture of people to make his promises come true. First God spoke to King Cyrus of Persia, who helped the Jews to go back and rebuild the temple. God gave Ezekiel a vision of the new temple, and told him exactly how it must be built. He told the people how they must worship in it. God sent Haggai and Zechariah to make sure the people did the work. He sent Nehemiah to make sure they rebuilt the walls of Jerusalem, and Ezra to remind them of the rules God had given them.

This all took many years. Many of the people never went back to Judah. Daniel was too old: he stayed in Persia. Others moved to Rome and Athens. God had promised a new beginning, but it would take years of hard work to make it come true.

Even after the temple was rebuilt, the people forgot his warnings. God used Malachi to warn them once again: 'A curse is on all of you because the whole nation is cheating me' (Malachi 3:9). Yes, there was more trouble to come, and more warnings.

STEP INTO THE FESTIVAL OF PURIM

The story of Esther, the Jewish orphan who became queen of Persia and saved the Jewish people from massacre, is celebrated each year at the Feast of Purim. 'Purim' means 'lots'—stones thrown like dice to decide on a date. It is celebrated by the Jews every spring, and is the scene of great fun and thanksgiving. Plan your own Purim party. It's traditional to wear fancy dress and masks, and to give gifts. Make the most of it!

GOD DELIVERS HIS PEOPLE ONCE AGAIN

King Xerxes of Persia was very cross. He called for his wife, and she wouldn't come. What a way to treat a king! He told his officials, 'Get rid of her. Find me a queen who'll do as she's told.' They found a beautiful young woman called Esther. Her cousin Mordecai worked for the king, but the king didn't know they were Jews.

One day the Prime Minister, Haman, declared that everyone should bow to him. Mordecai refused. He would bow to no one but God. Haman was furious. He gave orders for all the Jews to be killed, and threw lots to decide the date. Mordecai begged Esther to help the Jews. She was scared. It was against the law for her to go to the king un-invited. She asked all the Jews to fast and pray for three days, and promised to do the same. Then she would speak to the king, even if it meant her death.

Haman decided to hang Mordecai, and built the gallows outside his own home. To get the king into a good mood, Esther threw a party. The king loved it. In a happy mood, he remembered that he'd never rewarded Mordecai for once saving his life. He asked Haman's advice: how should he honour a good man? Haman thought the king meant him. He told the king to shower riches on him! Then he discovered that the king meant Mordecai. He was even more furious.

Esther threw another party for the king. She revealed Haman's plot to kill all the Jews. She told the king that she and Mordecai were Jews. The king heard about the gallows outside Haman's house. 'Hang Haman!' the king declared. And that was the end of Haman. The king could not cancel Haman's order to kill the Jews, but he made a law allowing them to defend themselves. On that day the Jews defeated all their enemies.

Mordecai decreed that every year the Jews should celebrate these events with feasts and parties, giving gifts to one another, and to the poor. We can still do the same. Jesus would have celebrated this festival every year.

STEP INTO THE SENSES

THE SENSE OF SIGHT

ESTHER'S SCROLL

The name of God does not appear in Esther's story, so the Jewish people can illustrate it on their scrolls without breaking the rule about not making an 'image' of God. Photocopy the story on page 68. Let the children mount it on their own 'scroll' and decorate its borders with pictures from the story.

MASKS

Make your own mask for the Purim party.

> *You will need stiff card, thin cord or elastic, scissors and materials to decorate.*

Cut a mask shape from stiff card, with holes for the eyes. Make a hole at each side and tie thin cord or elastic to fit around your head. Decorate it any way you like—with crayons, paints, fancy paper or glittering shapes. Be adventurous and add feathers or leaves.

paper fastener

I will turn their sorrow into gladness

I will turn their sorrow into gladness

fix at these corners with a dab of glue

SORROW INTO GLADNESS

> *You will need a piece of A5-sized stiff card plus a circle 9cm in diameter, colouring pencils or crayons, a small paper fastener.*

Fold the paper as illustrated above, and write on the words. Draw the face, and attach it with the fastener so that the paper will turn around. Attach a paperclip behind the top to make a wall hanging.

A STRANGE LAND

Invite the children to bring something from overseas which is strange to their culture. It may be a gift or something they've brought back from holiday. Talk about where it came from, what it is for, and its strangeness. If they had to spend a long time in a strange land, what would they like or not like about it?

THE SENSE OF SOUND

DROWN HIM OUT!

It is traditional that whenever Esther's story is read, at each mention of Haman's name everyone tries to blot it out by making a great noise, booing, hissing, and shaking *greggers* (rattles). Make *greggers* from a variety of tin and plastic containers filled with dried peas, pebbles, lentils and so on. Decorate them with coloured paper and ribbons.

SONGS OF HOME

When people move far away, they like to sing songs to remind them of home. Here are some examples:
• Scotland the brave
• Land of my fathers
• I'll take you home again, Kathleen
• The Lambeth walk
• On Ilkley Moor ba t'at

Can you think of any others? You could even practise some and give a concert to raise money for refugees.

SHALOM, MY FRIEND

Sing this sad song (JP217) thoughtfully. Remember as you sing that *shalom* means the deep peace of God.

FAMILIAR SOUNDS

Look at 'Home smells' on page 71. Do the same with sounds, but this time don't just name the sounds—make them.

THE SENSE OF TOUCH

CHAINS

Imagine how it must feel to be a prisoner in chains, as the people were who were taken to Bablyon.

> *You will need a piece of soft rope, a table set out with simple things to eat and drink, a basin with water, soap and a towel, a sleeping bag with pillow on the floor.*

Take turns to have your hands tied together with a soft rope. Try to do the things you would normally do, like eating and drinking, and going to bed. Imagine doing this all day and every day. Talk about how it feels.

GIFT BOXES

Purim is another great time of present-giving. Using the pattern on page 16, make cardboard boxes covered with patterned paper.

> *You will need stiff card, scissors, pencil, ruler.*

Mark the fold lines with the back of a scissors blade, but do not cut. This will make the card easier to fold. Make gift boxes to hold some gingerbread Hamans (see p. 72) to give as presents. Decorate them and tie with ribbon or fancy cord.

GOLD AND SILVER BOWLS

In Ezra 1, we read how King Cyrus sent the people back to Jerusalem to rebuild the temple. Look at the list of things he sent back with them (vv. 9–10). Make papier-mâché bowls, paint them gold or silver and give them as gifts.

> *You will need wallpaper paste, strips of newspaper, small bowls as models, oil.*

Grease the outside of your model bowl. Make up stiff wallpaper paste following the instructions on the packet. Paste about nine layers of newspaper over the bowl. Allow to dry, then paint.

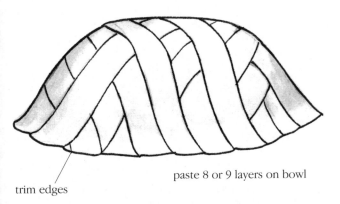

paste 8 or 9 layers on bowl

trim edges

THE SENSE OF SMELL

DANIEL'S DINNER

In Daniel 1:1–16, we read how Daniel wouldn't eat the king's meat. Invent your own recipe for a vegetarian meal you'd enjoy. Think about how it will smell. How about baked potato topped with baked beans or coleslaw? Cheese and tomato on toast? Or a vegetable stew different to Jacob's?

HOME SMELLS

What smells would you miss if you were far from home? Close your eyes and imagine walking through your house. Start in the bathroom… your favourite soap? Dad's shaving cream? In the

kitchen… toast under the grill? The smell of clean clothes being ironed? The lounge… your dog or cat? Your favourite cushion? The garden… someone cutting the grass? As you call them out, someone writes them down. See how long the list is. Go through again and see how many you think of the second time.

FIT FOR A QUEEN

Before Esther was made queen, she was given a whole year of beauty treatment and massaged with oils of myrrh and balsam. Try other essential oils such as cedarwood, cypress and frankincense. Mix a few drops with a spoonful of baby oil and try this on your wrists. Or use a modern perfumed body lotion.

THE SENSE OF TASTE

HAMAN'S EARS

Eating 'Haman's ears' is one of the treats of Purim. They are triangular pastries with sweet fillings.

> *You will need home-made or frozen sweet shortcrust pastry, and assorted fillings.*

Roll the pastry very thinly and cut into 8cm circles. Put a spoonful of filling in the centre and lift the sides to make a three-cornered shape. Seal the edges so that the filling doesn't leak. Bake for about 20 minutes at 190°C/Gas Mark 5.

Traditional fillings include honey and poppy seeds, but another tradition is the use of plum jam. You could use mincemeat, and add a spoonful of bread or cake crumbs to that or the jam to thicken it.

Warning: allow these pastries to cool before eating. The filling will be very hot.

GINGERBREAD HAMANS

These are good to make for presents.

You will need 120g each margarine and sugar (creamed together), 250g plain flour, plus 1 tsp each ginger and mixed spice (sifted together), 1 egg (beaten).

Combine egg with creamed mixture, then add flour and spices to make a firm dough. Shape by hand or cut with biscuit cutter, put on greased baking tray, and make eyes and mouth with currants and slivers of almond. Bake for about 18 minutes at 180°C/Gas Mark 5.

STEP INTO PRAYER

FOR REFUGEES

There are millions of refugees today. War, famine, floods or earthquakes are some of the causes.

You will need pictures from newspapers and magazines showing refugees.

Ask Oxfam and Tearfund for magazines. Cut pictures out and pin them on the walls.

Ask the children to imagine being without home, family, or security. Let them walk around the room and look at the pictures. Then ask them to draw a picture of one thing they would be sad to lose, such as a home or teddy bear, and tack it on the wall alongside one of the pictures. Then say this prayer:

Dear Father God, we thank you for all the things we have around us.
Familiar things. Comfortable things.
Things that make us feel happy and safe.
Please be with all those who have none of these things.
Send them the food and shelter they need,
And may they know your everlasting love.
Amen.

HERE I AM

Read Isaiah 65:1. Let the older children take turns to read the words aloud. What do we need that we haven't asked God for, in our group, our school, our town or our country?

Make a note of suggestions on a board, and read the list as a prayer.

STEP INTO THE EVERLASTING STORY

STEP INTO THE FUTURE

Have a look at the sky one clear night when the moon is full. The moon doesn't look far away, does it? It isn't. It's less than 385,000 km. The light of the moon reaches the earth in one and a quarter seconds. But many stars are so far away that it takes millions of years for their light to reach us. In fact, some of the stars began to shine before the earth was created!

The sky gives us some idea of how God sees things. Psalm 90 says, 'A thousand years to you are like one day.' In the Bible, God might be talking to the Israelites, to us, and people still to come, all at the same time. Mind-boggling, isn't it? Are those warnings and promises for the Israelites—or me?

Many of the warnings and promises have come true. God's people *did* go back to their land, and Jerusalem and the temple *were* rebuilt. But things went wrong again. Today the temple is no more, and there is fighting in the land of Israel.

Let's look at some of the second lot of exciting promises in Isaiah:

'A child is born to us! A son is given to us! And he will be our ruler. He will be called "Wonderful Counsellor", "Mighty God", "Eternal Father", "Prince of Peace"' (Isaiah 9:6).

'He was arrested and sentenced and led off to die, and no one cared about his fate. He was put to death for the sins of our people' (Isaiah 53:8).

Zechariah said, 'He comes triumphant and victorious, but humble and riding on a donkey' (Zechariah 9:9).

These words came true hundreds of years later. We can read all about them in Matthew, Mark, Luke and John. Yes, they are all part of the story of Jesus.

But many prophets were given a glimpse of the end of time, when Jesus will return. Jesus says that only God knows when this will happen. You could say the human race is now in extra time, even injury time. That's why Jesus told stories like the one about the servants being ready at all times. (Check God's promises in Isaiah 2:1–5; Joel 2:28–29 and Jeremiah 31:31–33.)

Some of the visions are alarming, but in Isaiah 54:11–13 God promises a new Jerusalem. In 65:17 he promises even more: 'I am making a new earth and new heavens. The events of the past will be completely forgotten.' With that promise, and the promise Jesus gave us, 'I will be with you always, to the end of the age', we have nothing to fear (Matthew 28:20).

STEP INTO THE FESTIVAL OF SHABBAT

SHABBAT

In Genesis 2:1–3 we see that a day of rest was part of God's creation plan. The Jewish people call this day Shabbat. We call it the Sabbath, or Sunday. God made it holy, and he told us in the fourth commandment to keep it holy.

The Israelites had very strict rules for keeping the Sabbath, and so do the Jewish people today. Sabbath begins on Friday evening. No work is done. All food must be cooked in advance and kept warm. The Sabbath is welcomed like a bride or a queen.

Think of ways you can make Sunday special. You could visit an elderly neighbour or phone someone you haven't seen for a while. Make a list of things you can do before Sunday, like finishing your homework or spending your pocket money.

WHAT THE LORD REQUIRES

In Micah 6:8, the prophet Micah says, 'The Lord has told us what is good. What he requires of us is this: to do what is just, to show constant love, and to live in humble fellowship with our God.' How can we make these words our rule for life today?

LOOKING FORWARD

However gloomy things look, never forget that promise, 'I will be with you always, to the end of the age' (Matthew 28:20).

Look back to the suggested preparations for the New Year on page 13. Make a shorter list, using the two headings 'Pray' and 'Get right with others', then add another: 'Read the Bible'.

Make your list in a notebook for the unknown future. You could look at it every new moon. (That's another festival the Jewish people were told to celebrate.)

STEP INTO THE SENSES

THE SENSE OF SIGHT

SHABBAT SHALOM

This traditional greeting means 'Sabbath peace'. In Isaiah 58:13–14 God says this about the Sabbath: 'If you treat the Sabbath as sacred and do not pursue your own interests on that day, if you value my holy day and honour it by not travelling, working, or talking idly on that day, then you will find the joy that comes from serving me.'

Lay a table the way it would be laid for a Sabbath meal, a very special family time. This would be Friday evening, after dark, so the candles are important.

> *You will need a clean white cloth, two or more candles, glasses, a bottle of juice, plates and cutlery, a plate of bread with a clean cover, and salt. (Learn how to fold a napkin attractively.)*

Even if you share only a piece of bread dipped in salt, and sip some juice, the candle-lit atmosphere should be special, and the candles, bread and wine may be blessed with the words, 'Blessed are you O Lord our God, King of the Universe, who gives us…'

A NEW JERUSALEM

Paint a frieze of the new Jerusalem.

> *You will need a very large piece of backing paper, a separate piece for each child, plus painting things and paste.*

Look at Isaiah 60, especially verses 1, 4, 6–9, 13, 15, 18–19 and 22. Ask the children to pick out one aspect of the new Jerusalem and paint a picture of it, then paste them all on one large sheet. If the younger children contribute no more than a smiling face, that is all right. Older children may like to paint the whole scene for themselves.

THE SENSE OF SOUND

GOD IS COMING

You will need trumpets (or equivalent), drums and tambourines.

Look at Joel 2.
- 'Blow the trumpet; sound the alarm on Zion, God's sacred hill' (2:1). *Sound the trumpets.*
- 'The Lord thunders commands to his army' (2:11). *Beat the drums.*
- 'Then the Lord showed concern for his land; he had mercy on his people' (2:18). *Sound the tambourines quietly.*
- 'Then, Israel, you will know that I am among you, and that I, the Lord, am your God and there is no other' (2:27). *Sound the tambourines slightly louder.*
- 'Afterwards I will pour out my Spirit on everyone:

your sons and daughters will proclaim my message; your old people will have dreams, and your young people will see visions' (2:28). *Play the tambourines louder still.*

SABBATH PRAYER

Listen quietly to the song 'Sabbath prayer' from the musical *Fiddler on the Roof*. These prayers are for daughters. Can the boys think of equivalent prayers for sons?

'AND THE GLORY OF THE LORD'

Play a recording of this chorus from Handel's *Messiah*. Compare the words of Isaiah 40:5 in the Good News Bible with Handel's score.

SOME SONGS TO SING

You may like to clap and dance to these songs.

Thank you, Lord, for this fine day (JP 232)
My Lord is higher than a mountain (JP170)
God is working his purpose out (verses 1 and 2) (MP189)

THE SENSE OF TOUCH

ANCIENT STONES

You will need a selection of fossils, rocks, coal, pumice and so on which are indisputably ancient.

Find out how old your samples are. Let the children hold them, and feel the texture and warmth.

If you have an ammonite or other fossil, close your eyes and imagine the kind of creature it once

was and the world it lived in. If you have pumice, imagine the lava that formed it, flowing from a volcano. With coal, imagine the prehistoric forest that made it. Enjoy a sense of continuity and God's view of time.

A BREAD COVER

It is traditional to cover the *challah* bread with a special cloth.

To make one, you will need a piece of fine-checked gingham about 33cm square (a square metre will make nine covers), blunt embroidery needle and coloured thread.

Either cut the square with pinking shears, or find a helper to machine-stitch the edges. Decide on a simple motif, perhaps a cross, a Star of David or *menorah*. Practise simple cross stitches before you begin, and don't pull them tight.

If you have time, embroider a cross-stitch border about 2cm from the edge.

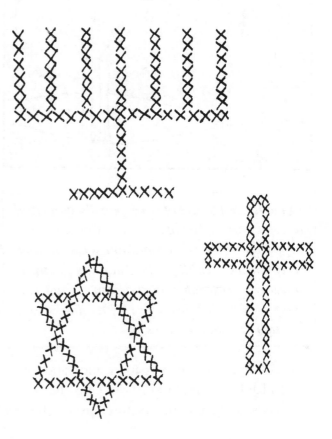

THE SENSE OF SMELL

SPICE BOXES

holes

Make boxes as for the gift boxes on page 16, but in an upright shape. Before sealing them, punch holes around the top so that the scent of the spices will escape. You can decorate these boxes to look like houses, castles, churches or anything you fancy.

Sprinkle an assortment of spices in the box and pass around so that everyone can enjoy the scent.

SPICE PICTURES

You will need pieces of card, pencils, glue, and a selection of whole spices. Choose from peppercorns, cloves, cinnamon sticks, sesame seed, allspice, chilli pepper, mace, star anise, mustard, coriander, cardamom, fenugreek, other seeds (see below). Use a glue strong enough to hold the spices.

Draw a simple picture, perhaps a landscape with a tree and animal. Paint over it with glue, then place the seeds to 'paint' the picture, using cheaper seeds like wheat, barley or lentils for the larger parts and spices to pick out the detail. You could use a pair of tweezers for this.

THE SENSE OF TASTE

THE SABBATH LOAF

It is traditional to make two special loaves of *challah* bread for the Sabbath, as reminders that God provided the Israelites with double portions of manna for the Sabbath. Use the recipe given for the New Year loaf on page 16, but make them in a plait shape as follows.

Divide each piece of dough into three and make long sausage shapes. Lay them alongside each other, and stick them together at one end with water. Now plait them as you would your hair, side-over-middle, then stick them together at the end.

Bake as for the New Year loaf. Put the dough in a hot oven, 200°C/Gas Mark 6, for one minute, then reduce to 180°C/Gas Mark 5 and bake for about 20-45 minutes, depending on size.

SALT

You will need some bread and a dish of salt.

It is traditional on the Sabbath to dip a piece of bread in salt before eating it. Salt is a good food preservative, and adds flavour. Jesus said that we must be like salt. Try this with whatever bread you have, and see what difference it makes.

Warning: eating too much salt is bad for your health.

STEP INTO PRAYER

A SABBATH BLESSING

You will need two candles, plus one for each child.

Someone lights the first candle and says, 'Lord, we thank you for the Sabbath, a day of rest. We welcome it. May it be a day of joy.' Someone lights the second candle  and says, 'Lord, we thank you for the Sabbath, a day of rest. We remember it. May it be a day of holiness.'

Each child now lights a candle for the next one and passes it to them, while everyone says, 'Lord, we thank you for… Please bless him/her.'

HAVDALAH

When three stars appear in the sky, the ceremony of *Havdalah* marks the end of Sabbath.

You will need red grape juice, a plate, glass and napkin, a small glass for each child, two candles and a spice box.

Let a child hold each of the candles. Stand the plate on a napkin and the glass on the plate. Someone holds the juice, and before pouring they say, 'Lord, we thank you for this juice, and for the Sabbath. May the joy of Sabbath pour over into the coming week.' Pour the juice and fill the glass to overflowing, so that it runs on to the plate.

Now give everyone a glass of juice and pass the spice box around for everyone to smell. With each sip of the juice, ask the children to pray for someone who has to work on the Sabbath—doctors, farmers, fire fighters and so on.

A BLESSING FOR ISRAEL

In Numbers 6:22–26, the Lord gave these words to Moses as a blessing for Israel. Write them on 6 cards:

May the Lord bless you
And take care of you;
May the Lord be kind
And gracious to you;
May the Lord look on you with favour
And give you peace.

Let the children read these lines in turn until they have learned them by heart. Use as a prayer spoken aloud for one another. Write the words on a prayer card to take home.

Section Two

STEP INTO THE STORIES
OF JESUS

STEP INTO THE STORY OF RE-CREATION

THE PARABLE OF THE SOWER

MARK 4:1–9

OLD TESTAMENT LINK

The kingdom of God is fulfilled by the work of God himself.

(This parable can also be read with sound effects! See 'Let's hear it for the farmer!' activity on page 85.)

The crowd gathered beside Lake Galilee was *huge*! Jesus wanted to talk to the people, but there was barely space for him to stand, let alone be seen by everyone. So, what did he do? He climbed into a small boat at the water's edge and rowed out a little way from the shore. That was better! Now he could certainly see everyone, and they could certainly see him!

He gazed at their expectant faces. Men and women—lots of children, too—all waiting for him to teach them about God. On this particular day he wanted to explain how important it is to learn about the kingdom of God—to make sure that the words we hear 'take root' in our hearts, and don't get choked up with all the other things going on in our lives. Now Jesus' favourite way of explaining things was to tell stories, so he decided to compare someone who teaches about God with someone scattering seeds in a field, and this was the story he told. One day, a farmer went out to scatter seed in one of his fields. He grabbed his sack and headed off down the road. Unfortunately, he didn't notice that there was a little hole in the sack, which meant that, on the way, some of the seeds fell on the pathway. Now that wasn't any good for growing seeds, but it was very handy for some hungry birds in a nearby tree. 'Instant food,' they thought, 'what luck!' and swooped down to gobble up the whole lot in five minutes flat.

Never mind, there were still lots of seeds left. The busy farmer stood in the middle of the field, plunged his hand in the sack and pulled out handful after handful, scattering the seeds all around. When the sack was empty, he tucked it under his arm, and hurried off to get on with the next job.

He'd just left the field when, unfortunately, a gust of wind came and blew some of the seeds on to a patch of ground that was actually very rocky, with just a thin layer of soil on top. Never mind, within a week those seeds did start sprouting very quickly, which was brilliant! But then, because the new shoots were in such a little bit of earth and had hardly any roots, as soon as the sun began shining they quickly got scorched, dried up, and died. Not so brilliant! More of the seeds lost.

Now, that really hadn't been a good day for the farmer, because what he didn't notice was that another lot of seeds fell where thorn bushes were just beginning to sprout. This meant that, although the seeds began growing quite nicely, with good roots, they didn't grow as fast as the thorn bushes. The new little plants got completely choked, and never in the end managed to produce any grain at all. So that was another load of seeds gone to waste.

But now for the good news! Some of the seeds *did* fall on good ground. Those plants grew beautifully, and produced thirty, or sixty, or even a hundred times as many seeds as had originally been scattered.

Jesus, having finished his story, looked slowly around at the huge crowd. He had a wonderful way of making everyone feel he was looking at them and them alone. He smiled, then called out, 'You have listened to me, I know, but have you really *heard and understood* what I have said?'

STEP INTO THE SENSES

THE SENSE OF SIGHT

MATCH THE WORDS

This activity will remind the children what happened to the seeds, and what that meant.

You will need four large, colourful pictures, using the simple illustrations shown below.

Fix the pictures to four sides of the room and remind the children what each picture means.

- The birds pecking at the seeds = God's word being snatched away.
- The withered plants on the rocks = the message not taking root.
- The plants among the thorn bushes = the word being choked out.
- The straight and strong plants = God's word being heard and understood.

When a leader calls out, 'God's word… ', followed by, '…is snatched away!', '…has no roots!', '…is choked out!' or '…is heard and understood!', the children have to run as quickly as they can to the picture that matches the phrase.

If there's a large group of children, the last one to reach the correct picture can be called 'Out!' Otherwise, the children can just have fun trying to reach each place first.

MAKE YOUR VERY OWN FARMER'S FIELD

You will need one shallow plastic tray per child (or a large one that the group can work on together), slightly dampened soil, lots of small stones, some large stones, lots of small broken twigs, cress seeds.

- For the good part of the field: working diagonally, corner to corner, fill half the tray with some soil, to about 15mm depth.
- For the pathway: using lots of small stones, make a diagonal path across the tray.
- For the rocky section: using larger stones, fill half the remaining space, putting a bit of dampened soil on top of the stones.
- For the thorny bushes: fill the other half of that space with a little damp soil, and lots of small twigs sticking up.
- Let the children scatter some cress seeds over the whole of their field.
- The children should keep their 'fields' in a warm, light, airy place, watering them lightly, then report in the following weeks how their seeds are progressing.
- If one large 'field' has been created, this needs to be kept somewhere where the children can check on it each week to see how the seeds are growing.

THE SENSE OF SOUND

WHISPERING THE WORD

Jesus was wonderful at explaining things, but we're not so good at it. Sometimes the message just doesn't get through as well as it should.

You will need cards with each of the following messages written on, plus some blank sheets of paper.

- *Message One: Jesus is my best friend—and yours, too!*
- *Message Two: God never breaks a promise.*
- *Message Three: Jesus says I'm great. Isn't that just great?*

Divide the children into three groups. Give the first in each group a card with one of the messages to whisper into the ear of the next child, who then whispers it to the next, and so on down the line. (Keep just one group if you have very few children.)

When it reaches the end of the line, a leader should write down what the last child in the row thinks the message is. When everyone's finished, the messages can be read out, to see how much they've (probably!) changed.

LET'S HEAR IT FOR THE FARMER!

The parable can be made more exciting to listen to if the following sound effects are added. The children can either close their eyes and listen while the leaders make the sounds, or older children can be given a sound effect to make at the appropriate time.

You will need:

- *Uncooked rice or dry beans in a plastic box: shake, for the seeds being scattered.*
- *Your own voice or a small whistle: for bird noises.*
- *Elastic band stretched around a ruler: when pinged, it makes a nice pecking sound!*
- *Large piece of cardboard: waved around, you'll feel, as well as hear, the wind blowing!*
- *Small box filled with stones: to be shaken, for the seeds landing on the rocks.*
- *Large plastic bag: to be rustled, for the plants growing quickly.*
- *Blown-up balloon: to pop, for the plants suddenly shrivelling up and dying in the sun.*
- *Rough sandpaper: rub two bits together for a scraping noise, for thorn bushes growing.*
- *Paper: screw up and rub on the sandpaper, for plants growing among thorn bushes.*
- *Balloon pump: push in and out, for a nice 'plant-growing' sound.*
- *Large packet of seeds: shake, for all the seeds made from the plants in the good soil.*

THE SENSE OF TOUCH

ALL CHANGE!

The farmer planted seeds in his field, hoping they would change into something completely different —which some of them, of course, did! Here are a few simple experiments, changing one thing into another, which the children can both watch and help with, and experience how each of the new substances *feels*.

Changing liquid into solid

Warm some creamy milk in a saucepan. When it's just simmering, slowly stir in a few teaspoons of vinegar. Keep stirring until it becomes rubbery. Let it cool, then wash it under running water. The result should be a lump of 'plastic', which can be moulded into shapes, and even bounced around!

Changing powder into a solid, then back again

Mix some cornflour with water. By varying the quantities of each, the mixture can be very solid one moment, then very runny the next. If the mixture is made halfway between the two, and you tap your finger on the top, it will feel quite solid, yet if you stir your finger around, it will suddenly be far more runny!

Changing liquid into solid

Using a bottle of liquid-chocolate sauce, squeeze some into a see-through jug containing icy water. Suddenly, the liquid chocolate becomes a solid!

CUT IT OUT!

Ask the children to close their eyes and imagine they're in the garden, scattering seeds like the farmer did. It's spring, and the sun is shining. What can they see as they look around? Trees… birds… flowers… insects… lots of other things beside! It's easy to tell what these things are when we can see them, but how about if we can only *feel* them?

You will need:
- *Some items from a garden, such as flowers, stones, twigs, weeds, an apple, grass, ivy, and so on, and add any toy insects or birds that are available. (You could add to these some cardboard cut-outs of any of the illustrations shown below, prepared beforehand or made by the children as part of the activity.)*
- *A box to put the items in, with cut-out openings in both sides large enough to extract any one of the contents.*

Each child in turn runs up to the box, and reaches both hands inside to pick up and feel one of the items inside. They must quickly say what they think it is, then pull it out. If they've got the answer right, they get a big cheer and the item is removed from the box. If they're wrong, it must go back in. How quickly can they empty the box?

THE SENSE OF SMELL

FOLLOW YOUR NOSES!

Maybe Jesus thought of this parable because he knew a farmer who'd had this much trouble getting his seeds to grow. Perhaps it had been an especially windy day, or maybe the farmer couldn't see too well—perhaps not even at all—and just had to hope that some of the seeds ended up in the right place. If you can't see well, it's wonderful how other senses become stronger. You learn to use your nose much more, for a start! If the farmer had been able to find the good part of the field by something he could *smell*, that would have helped a lot.

You will need four cards (at least A4 size), four perfumed sprays (each with a different scent), a plant or bunch of flowers, some weeds, a few large stones, and a piece of sandpaper (for the path), plus a box to put each item in.

Draw on each card a simple picture of each part of the field. Spray the back of each card with one of the different perfumes, making sure the children don't see which spray is used for which card. Prop each card on a chair, picture-side hidden, with one of the boxes underneath the chair, making sure that what the box contains matches what is on the card.

Spray the children's wrists with the spray for the good part of the field, then ask them to smell each of the four cards and stand by the one they think has the matching smell. When they've made their choice, they can open the box and see if it was the right one! Repeat for one or two more of the other smells, using different wrists and backs of hands to avoid a confusion of smells.

POST IT!

This activity is a little more difficult. How good is each child's sense of smell?

You will need:
- *Small envelopes—sealed, but with a gap at the top for smelling the following contents: dry soil, sand, weeds, a flower, uncooked rice, dry porridge oats, cornflakes, dry beans, bread and puffed wheat cereal. (NB: Make a secret mark on each envelope indicating its contents.)*
- *Empty cereal packets, or similar cardboard boxes, with the name of each of the above marked on the outside, left open at the top, or with a 'post hole' cut in the front.*

Divide the children into small groups (depending on the number of children present). Give the first group one of the envelopes each and tell them to smell the contents, then post them into whichever box they think is the right one, as quickly as possible. Check to see how many got their smells right, then repeat with the next group of children.

THE SENSE OF TASTE

TASTE AND SEE

Sharing food with other people, especially those who haven't much of their own, is an important way of getting God's message of love across. But the food has to be good to taste—just like God's love. And the message must be a true one.

Imagine if we gave someone old brown bananas with lots of thick gravy, but said they were delicious sausages. They might believe us until they tasted the food. Then they'd know the truth! Or would they? The children probably think they could easily tell the difference between fudge and frankfurters, but they might be surprised. As Jesus explained, getting the message across isn't always easy.

You will need plates with small pieces of any of the following: fruit, cooked sausage or frankfurters, cheese, white and milk chocolate, fudge, and so on.

Ask the children to close their eyes, then pop in their mouths a piece of one of the above, but tell them it's one of the other flavours. (You can tell them all the same thing, or say something different for each—even mentioning the correct flavour to one or two!)

Then ask them to say what they thought they were eating. How many got it right? Repeat for two or three other flavours.

THE BREAD OF LIFE

Jesus chose this story to explain about God's kingdom, because food, like God's word, is vital for our survival. That's why the word of God is so often called the bread of life. But, like God's word, we often take something as 'basic' as bread for granted.

You will need as many different types of bread as you can find. Choose from white and granary, but also French baguette, Italian ciabatta and foccacia, Greek pitta bread, Indian naan, and so on. Break them up into bite-sized pieces.

Ask the children to close their eyes, and hand around one type of bread at a time. Did they like that flavour/texture? When they've tasted them all, did they have a favourite? Did they realize there were so many different types of bread? What sort of bread would Jesus have eaten? (It would have been rather like the pitta.)

STEP INTO REFLECTION

A little bit later on in Mark 4 (verses 13–20), Jesus explains to the disciples exactly what the parable meant. Here's what he said:

- The seeds that landed on the path are like people who are told about God and Jesus. But they don't pay much attention, and quickly forget, so that it's easy for the message to be stolen away from them.

- The seeds that fell on rocky ground are like people who hear about God and think he's really great! But they don't try to learn more, and their faith doesn't go very deep, so it never gets any 'roots'. Then, as soon as life gets difficult, or their belief loses them friends or causes them any trouble, they give it all up.

- The seeds that fell among the thorny bushes are also like people who hear about God and Jesus, but spend so much time worrying about their work, and making money, and trying to get everything they want, that they leave no time for God. His message gets choked out by everything else in their lives, so that their own faith never grows, and they don't spread the great news of God's love to anyone else, either.

- The seeds that fell on good ground are like the people who hear and welcome everything they hear about God. They give him their time and enthusiasm, and go on to learn much more. And, because they've grown in faith so much, they're then able to spread God's word to thirty or sixty, or even a hundred other people!

Just imagine that Jesus has *this very minute* walked into the room. He's sitting down in front of you and he wants to tell you one of his wonderful parables. Of course, because this is the 21st century, he'll talk about something much more modern than wandering around a field scattering seeds! Maybe he'll tell a story to do with computer games; being invited to a party; choosing which movie to go and see, or video to watch at home; playing football; space travel; or, perhaps, learning how to do some-thing you've never tried before.

As a group, or in pairs, create your own up-to-date parable for this message, which Jesus might tell today.

SOME QUESTIONS

- How do you think you can be more like the seed that falls on the good ground?
- What can you do to learn more about Jesus and God?
- How much do you think that would help make your life better?

You can ask Jesus for his help at any time—he's always listening. Perhaps you can think of a prayer you'd like to say right now. There are also some on the next two pages that you can read out loud.

STEP INTO PRAYER

JESUS TALKED TO ME TODAY...

*...but some of the words got all muddled and tangled up in my head
and I didn't understand what was said. Sorry!
Then I think Jesus said something good,
but I was a bit busy wondering what was for lunch and
if Mum'd let me watch a video after school or take me to the park.
So I forgot what you said, Jesus. Sorry!*

*Then I was trying to listen. I really was.
But a little voice inside my head kept saying, 'That's not true. Don't believe a word of it.'
And then I didn't know what to think, Jesus. Sorry!*

*But I've just heard you say that you love me. Really, really, really love me.
Wow! I heard that! So that's one seed that's got planted, Jesus.
I think I'd better look after this one and make sure it grows tall and strong,
with a terrific great flower that everyone can see. Called me!*

PRAYER WITH ACTIONS

Children form a circle, starting each verse tightly curled on the floor. Put actions to words according to ability. Finish standing straight and tall in their circle, with arms upwards, holding each other's hands.

I'm just a little seed but I really want to grow...
TALL and STRAIGHT and FINE and STRONG
but something seems to have gone wrong.
I'm falling, falling, falling
down on to the road.
And I can see a crow,
swooping low.
And now
I know
that
I won't
grow.

I'm just a little seed but I really want to grow...
FINE and STRONG and STRAIGHT and TALL
but I can see I'm going to fall
down and down and down
on to some rocks.
But there is some soil, so I'll start to grow,
and the sun shines bright so I'll grow some more.
But it's too hot, and the roots I've got
are far too small.
So now I know
that I shan't
grow.

I'm just a little seed, but I really want to grow...
FINE and STRONG and TALL and STRAIGHT.
I'm falling now. I just can't wait!
The ground round here looks pretty good. I'm doing
fine. I knew I could!
But ouch! and ow! and ouch again!
There's spikes and thorns.
My roots are torn.
And now I know
that I can't
grow.

I'm just a little seed, but I really want to grow...
TALL and STRONG and STRAIGHT and FINE
and I've landed where the sun will shine.
The earth looks good, I'm doing great! My roots go deep. I'm tall and straight.
I'm strong. And look at all my shoots—and all my seeds—and all my fruit!
With Jesus' help, I'll multiply. With Jesus' help, I'll reach the sky.
And now I know that I can GROW and GROW and GROW and GROW and GROW!

Chapter 12

STEP INTO THE STORY OF RESCUE

THE PARABLE OF THE LOST SHEEP

LUKE 15:4–7

OLD TESTAMENT LINK

God actively seeks out and rescues his people.

The activity 'Can you get your sheep home?' on page 93 could be used before telling this parable.

One of the most special things about Jesus is that, although he was perfect in every way, he chose to spend his time with ordinary people who, like us, got a lot of things wrong a lot of the time. And he wanted to let them—and us—know that even though we're never going to manage to be perfect, God will always care about every single one of us and will never, ever give up on us. In short, he loves us to bits! While you listen to or read this parable, you need to know that *God* is the shepherd and *you* are that one lost sheep!

Now this particular shepherd, Jesus said, had lots of sheep—one hundred, to be exact. He'd given them all names and knew them so well that he could easily recognize one from the other. Each day he'd take the flock to a different part of the hillside so that they had fresh grass to eat, and count them often to make sure they were all safe and sound. He'd sometimes have to risk his own life to protect them from dangerous wild animals like wolves or hyenas, or poisonous snakes and scorpions, and even nasty men who might try to steal some of his precious flock. Then, at the end of each day, he'd happily drive his hundred sheep back down the hill to the night-time safety of their sheep-pen.

But then one day an awful thing happened. The shepherd was counting his sheep and only got as far as 99! He counted again, but there was no mistake. Charlie, the youngest, and always mischievous, was definitely missing. Making sure the others were safe, he climbed to the top of the hill and looked all around, but there was no sign of Charlie anywhere.

The shepherd searched the whole, hot day, getting more and more worried, and more and more exhausted. By the time the sun had set, his feet were covered in blisters from all the walking; his legs covered in scratches from clambering through thick brambles; his knees covered in bruises from falling over rocks and boulders; and his stomach was making an awful noise, because he was now extremely hungry. And still no sign of Charlie.

So did he give up? Did he say to himself, 'It doesn't matter, I've still got 99 other sheep. I just won't bother about Charlie any more'? No, he certainly didn't! He kept on looking, right through the night, until at last, just as the sun was rising, he found his lost sheep—down the bottom of a deep gully, uninjured, but stuck up to its tummy in thick,

gooey mud! Charlie, hearing the shepherd and knowing he was at last going to be rescued, bleated loudly. For a while there, he'd thought he would never get out!

Using the long rope he'd brought with him, attaching one end to a nearby tree-trunk, the shepherd lowered himself down the gully, then somehow managed to get himself and Charlie back up to safety. Forgetting his tiredness and delightedly lifting his muddy sheep on to his shoulders, he merrily carried it all the way back to the rest of his flock. And then the shepherd invited all his family and friends round to his home to celebrate with him that he had found his precious —and irreplaceable—lost sheep.

Jesus says that there are celebrations just like that in heaven when anyone decides to believe in God. No matter how many other people believe, God is still thrilled to welcome another person into his family because, like Charlie the sheep, every one of us is special and valuable.

STEP INTO THE SENSES

THE SENSE OF SIGHT

CAN YOU GET YOUR SHEEP HOME?

Every evening the shepherd had to herd his 100 sheep back into the safety of their pen. How easy will the children find it to get their sheep home?

> *You will need:*
> - *Something to create an opening into two 'sheep pens'. These could be made out of large cardboard boxes, with both ends open to form a tunnel (the area beyond which would be 'the pen'). Or use chairs, with their backs towards each other and a sheet draped over, to form the tunnel.*
> - *Cut-outs of as many sheep as the group needs (using illustration below as a guide).*
> - *Two rolled-up newspapers.*

Create two tunnels, and divide the children into two teams. By flapping their rolled-up newspapers, the children have to guide their sheep through the tunnel and out the other side, before they can be considered safely 'in their pen'. Set the distance to 'the pen' dependent on the age of the children. Each child, when running back to his/her team, must hand over the newspaper to the child at the front of the team, for their turn.

MEMORY GAME

The shepherd remembered all 100 of his sheep's names. How good are the children's memories for names?

> *You will need a large sheet and a collection of cuddly toys (the younger the children, the fewer the toys), each with a name attached. The more inventive the names, the better!*

Spread the toys out on a table, covered with a sheet. Remove the sheet and give the children about three minutes to try to memorize all the names (if possible, use a timer, or ring a bell when the time is up). Then put back the sheet.

Get the children to call out all the names they remember, with one of the leaders bringing out from under the sheet all those which are correctly remembered.

For older children, there could be the added challenge of seeing if they can remember which cuddly toy had which name!

THE SENSE OF SOUND

MATCH THE SOUND

The poor lost sheep was probably bleating as loudly as it possibly could, hoping the shepherd would hear it and come to its rescue. How well can the children recognize sounds and then figure out where they're coming from?

Give all but one of the children a simple 'animal' sound to make (for example, sheep, pig, dog, cat, cow, horse, mouse, monkey, chicken, turkey, cockerel). Stand the remaining child in the middle of the room, blindfold him or her (checking first that s/he is happy for you to do this) and say which of the allocated animals s/he will be searching for.

Seat the other children on chairs in a circle around the central child (the smaller the circle, the more difficult this is to do). They then make their animal noises all at the same time and, while remaining in the middle of the circle, the blindfolded child has to try to point in the direction of the right noise (a time limit can be put on this).

When the choice has been made—correctly or otherwise—the child with the actual matching sound swaps with the one in the middle, and the whole thing is repeated.

MAKING MUSIC!

Jesus tells us that there are celebrations in heaven, which is good to know, because most of us like having parties—especially with lots of loud music! This activity helps the children to use their imagination and ingenuity to make their very own unique 'music'!

You will need:
- *A selection of the following: metal trays, saucepan lids, wooden spoons, plastic bottles filled to different levels with water or soil, old coffee mugs, containers of uncooked rice/beans, metal spoons, whisks, bowls, old ballpoint pens, bottle tops, empty cans, cardboard tubes and boxes, rulers, lots of elastic bands, plastic flower pots, foil containers, old toothbrushes, coins and so on.*
- *A list of familiar songs and tunes.*

Give each child or group of children one tune to try to recreate, using their choice of 'instruments'. After a bit of practice they can perform their song to the others. Can anyone recognize the tunes?

THE SENSE OF TOUCH

PUTTING CHARLIE SAFELY BACK TOGETHER AGAIN

You will need one large card with a simple outline of a sheep (see page 93), a blindfold, and duplicate cut-outs of the various parts of a sheep—four legs, two ears, two eyes, a nose and a tail (stick some cotton wool on the tail piece of card)—with a piece of Blu-tack stuck to the back of each one.

Set the large card up at eye-level in front of the children. In turn, while blindfolded, they try to stick each part of Charlie on to the right place.

If there are not too many children in the group, they can each have all the pieces to stick on in one go. With more children, they can have one part each and take it in turns, so the finished picture is a joint production—and probably a most interesting one!

HELP ME FIND MY WAY HOME

You will need several blindfolds, and items to create an obstacle course, with a specific 'home' base. Use such things as chairs, tables, brooms or mops to step over, a pile of blankets, a small ladder and so on.

Children should be divided into pairs, one of whom (the sheep) will be blindfolded. The children without the blindfolds are the shepherds and must help the others, with spoken instructions and gentle guiding, to feel their way through the obstacle course and get safely 'home'. The course can be as simple or difficult as the ages of the children warrant.

The pairs can then be swapped around and the course altered for the new 'sheep'. Afterwards, the children can be encouraged to say how they felt about being unable to see, having to rely on their sense of touch, and having to trust their safety to someone else.

NB: Please make sure that the 'shepherds' guide their partners carefully and safely, while at the same time allowing the 'sheep' to feel their own way.

THE SENSE OF SMELL

SMELLY SHEEP!

Sheep have a very distinctive smell. If they all smelt of something different, lost ones might be easier to find. Or would they? With this activity, the children discover the answer!

> *You will need lumps of cotton wool, soaked in some or all of the following: bath oil, vinegar, almond essence, vanilla essence, mint flavouring, coffee, cocoa, orange squash, pineapple juice, and so on.*

Place the soaked cotton wool on saucers at the beginning of the activity, lightly covering each one with tissue paper so that no giveaway colour can be seen. Place the saucers around the room, making sure you know exactly which is which! Whisper to each child one of the following facts about the sheep they're trying to find:

'The sheep you are looking for... has had a nice bath / is very nutty! / has eaten fish and chips and spilt the vinegar / has just eaten some vanilla ice-cream / loves peppermints / likes coffee / is a chocoholic / has eaten a pineapple', and so on.

The children have to see if they can find the correct 'sheep' smell, and stand by the saucer that they think is the right one. The children who have found the correct smell can be congratulated! Repeat as many more times as wished.

A SMELLY INVITATION

The shepherd would just have had to knock on a few doors to invite his friends and neighbours to help him celebrate finding his lost sheep but, if you want to hold a party today, you need to send out invitations.

> *You will need plain card or sheets of paper (folded so that they stand up), felt-tipped pens, crayons, and so on, lumps of cotton wool, the liquids used for 'Smelly Sheep', glue.*

The children can each make an invitation card, illustrating it with something out of the story, and incorporating the cotton wool, stuck on to the card, as part of a sheep, tree, bush, shepherd's clothing, and so on. They can then choose which smell they'd like dabbed on to the cotton wool, to make a nice smelly invitation!

THE SENSE OF TASTE

Celebrations in heaven must be really spectacular. But whether there's food to taste is another matter altogether! Here on earth, though, when any of us celebrate anything at all, we usually expect to have nice things to eat and drink. So, to celebrate the fact that God loves us, whoever we are, the children can quickly make these cookies to eat, followed by a tasting game that they should enjoy.

ICED BISCUITS

You will need:
- *Sweet biscuits, like digestives or plain tea biscuits, and/or crackers, for a less-sweet alternative.*
- *200g (8oz) icing sugar, 2–4 tbsp warm water, food colouring and small sweets for decoration.*
- *Large mixing bowl and two or three smaller bowls.*

1. Mix the icing sugar and water together in the larger bowl.
2. Divide the mixture between the smaller bowls, with a different food colouring in each.
3. Spoon half a teaspoon of icing on to each biscuit, and spread as evenly as possible.
4. If using crackers, spread a teaspoon of icing on two, then sandwich together, putting a little more icing on the top.
5. Before the icing sets on the top of the biscuits, decorate with the sweets.

TASTE THE DIFFERENCE!

You will need:
- *Half a dozen different flavours of crisps.*
- *Orange, blackcurrant, pineapple and apple juice, in containers which are almost completely covered over with card and sticky tape (hiding the colour of the juice, but allowing room to insert a straw).*
- *Drinking straws.*
- *A checklist of the flavours, so that the children can put a number on their sheet against the flavour they think they're tasting.*

Arrange the crisps and drinks alternately along a table, numbered one to ten.

The children can then work their way along the table, writing down what they think the flavours are. At the end, they can discover who's got the most sensitive taste buds!

STEP INTO REFLECTION

The shepherd could have kept his one hundred sheep much safer if he'd left them in the pen all the time. If they hadn't had the freedom to wander around, none would ever have got lost, or hurt or stolen. So why didn't the shepherd do that? Ask the children what they think, and whether, if they'd been the shepherd, they'd have let their sheep roam about.

God is a wonderful shepherd, looking after all of us (his sheep) but, like the shepherd in the parable, he doesn't keep us locked up in a small, safe place. Instead, he gives us freedom to go where we choose and do what we want. Why does God do that? Just like the shepherd, he could choose to give us no freedom at all and so stop us ever getting hurt or doing things wrong. Ask the children which they would prefer.

Do they agree with how much freedom God gives us, even though it means that life is more dangerous and bad things can happen because we're allowed the 'freedom' to hurt each other?

A STORY

There were once two lovely, fluffy, snow-white toy gorillas (that growled when their tummies were squeezed!), sitting on a shelf in a toy shop waiting to be bought. One day two children went into the shop with their mums, and were each bought one of the toys.

Now the first child, when she got home, looked at the soft, white fur of the gorilla and thought, 'If I play with this it's going to get all dirty, and bits of its fur might rub off. It'll be much better if I leave it in its box and put it on a shelf and just look at it, but never play with it.' So that's exactly what she did.

But the second child, when he got home, looked at the soft, white fur of his gorilla and thought, 'That's going to make a great pillow tonight, and I can't wait to make it growl at all my friends! Then when I go on holiday next week it'll come, too, and I'll take it to grandad's on Sunday, and it can sit on my lap when I have tea today!' And that's exactly what he did.

Two years later, the first gorilla was still sitting up on the shelf in its box. It was just as soft and cuddly and white as the day it had been bought, but no one had ever felt how soft and cuddly it was, and no one could even see how white it was, because the box was now covered in a thick layer of dust. And no one had ever, ever heard it growl.

The second gorilla, however, was really quite a sorry sight! Its fur—what little there was of it—was now a dingy grey, and one of its eyes had fallen out months before, but it still made a great pillow every night. Wherever the boy went, the toy still went too, and when he felt (as he sometimes did) that he hadn't a friend in the world, the gorilla growled in sympathy as best it could, though its batteries had all but run out. In fact, that gorilla had been loved so much, it was practically real.

If the children could be either toy, which would they want to be?

REFLECTION

It's because God loves us so much that he gives us the freedom to live our lives to the full, even though that means we are not always safe from dangers and troubles.

But, whatever happens to us, God is always there beside us, ready to help whenever we ask.

STEP INTO PRAYER

It would be nice to give the angels an excuse
to have a party!

If I were an angel
I'd hope that someone
down here
would say,
'Hey, I think God's great!'
and, 'Jesus is pretty cool, too!'

And then me,
and the rest of the angels,
could whiz around
and blow up balloons—
or clouds, maybe—
and decorate the sky with a rainbow,
and eat angel cake
and specially prepared loaves and fishes
(sprinkled with hundreds and thousands)
and play our harps
REALLY LOUD!
and have a great time
CELEBRATING
'cos someone decided to believe in God.

Yes, it would be nice to give the angels an excuse to have a party.

Children who are old enough can be encouraged to create their own prayer.

The prayers could be written on card or paper to be taken home. One could be chosen, perhaps at random, to be used as a prayer to finish with.

Chapter 13

STEP INTO THE STORY OF GOD'S GOODNESS

THE PARABLE OF THE FRIEND AT MIDNIGHT

LUKE 11:5–8

OLD TESTAMENT LINK

God wants us to receive good things.

If people didn't do *exactly* what God wanted, he'd punish them—well, that was what people in Jesus' day were taught to believe. They thought that if they became ill, couldn't walk, or were deaf or blind, it was because they—or even their parents or grandparents—had done some very wrong things and God was making them suffer because of it.

But Jesus knew that this just wasn't true. Although bad things do happen to us all sometimes, because we're not living in a perfect world,

God loves us far too much to want to make bad things happen. So, time for a parable! And Jesus wants us, 2000 years later, to get the message, too. It's important to remember that in Jesus' day there were no phones, cars, buses or trains. There were no fridges, freezers, electric ovens, microwaves or supermarkets. People baked their own bread, milked their own cows and grew their own vegetables.

It's midnight. Jacob is fast asleep on the floor (no nice comfortable beds, in those days). His home is a flat-roofed, two-roomed house that he shares with three generations of his family. Suddenly, everyone is woken by someone knocking loudly at the door. Amazingly, they discover it's a friend they haven't seen for ages and ages and certainly weren't expecting to see in the middle of the night! Jacob realizes that their friend is very hungry, but

oh no! The bread, and vegetable stew that Mum had made for supper that night has all been eaten. What's in the store cupboard? Only a small sack of grain, some sour milk that's just about turned to cheese, some dried peas and lentils and a few olives. Nothing much for a weary traveller among that lot! 'Never mind!' Mum says. 'Go to our friendly neighbour and ask to borrow three loaves of bread. At least that'll be something to put with the cheese.'

'But it's the middle of the night—they'll all be asleep!' Jacob protests. 'Can't someone else go?' He looks hopefully around at the others, but no one else is offering. So out he goes, into the darkness, across to the next house. He knocks on the door. It sounds terribly loud in the silent night, but he gets no answer, so he knocks again. Suddenly one of the window shutters opens a little, and Jacob sees their (normally) friendly neighbour peering sleepily out.

'Er… sorry to disturb you,' he says, 'but a friend has come to visit and we've got nothing to give him to eat. Can we borrow three loaves of bread, please?'

Their normally friendly neighbour isn't too impressed! 'It's the middle of the night! The door is bolted, my children and I are in bed so, no, I can't get up to give you anything. Go away and don't bother me!' And with that, he slams the shutter closed.

What's poor Jacob going to do now? He can't go back empty-handed. There's nothing else for it but

to ask again. So he knocks once more. Once more he gets refused, so he tries a third time and, to his great relief, this time the door opens and there is their neighbour—not only with three loaves of bread, but also holding a basket containing a nice juicy melon, a couple of dried, salted fish, and a full jug of wine. 'Here you are,' he grins, holding the basket out to Jacob. 'Sorry I didn't take you seriously at first. But you weren't afraid to keep on asking, so I knew you really needed the bread—and probably a lot more besides!'

How much more, Jesus says, will God be ready to give you exactly what you really need, because he only wants us to have good things. All you have to do is ask!

STEP INTO THE SENSES

THE SENSE OF SIGHT

HAVE YOU GOT WHAT I NEED?

One of the most important things Jesus wanted to encourage us to do was to help each other, and to share what we have with other people.

You will need:
- *A simple outline drawing of some of the following: an apple, potato, carrot, sausages, pear, cheese, eggs, mushrooms, banana, onion, fish, cake, biscuits, bottle of fruit juice.*
- *The above food items—the real thing or an empty packet/box would do fine. (Have more items than there are children in the group.)*
- *A simple disguise for one of the leaders, making them look like a poor old man or woman.*
- *A box or basket for the food items to be put in.*

Fix the pictures on to the seat side of the chairs, spaced as evenly as possible around the edges of the room, chairs facing inwards, with the relevant food item on the seat of each chair. The disguised leader hobbles into the room and calls out, 'I need sausages', or, 'Have you got any potatoes?', 'I'd love an apple', and so on.

The children run to the appropriate picture and queue up behind that chair. Whoever was first to the correct picture takes the food item and keeps hold of it—but remember, the more each one 'wins', the harder it'll be to keep hold of everything!

The leader calls out for another item, and again the first child to queue up behind the chair takes the food item. When everything has been called out, the items are carried over to the 'old' man or woman and put in their basket or box.

YOUR GOOD DEED

Jesus spent his life doing the best he possibly could for the people he met, and he promises us that God only wants to give us good things, too. He asks us to do the same for each other. Encourage the children to think of ways of helping other people—starting today!

You will need sheets of paper folded six times like a thick fan, with a figure drawn on the top panel, several pairs of scissors, plus pens, crayons, or pencils.

The children cut from their sheets of folded paper a linked row of paper people. (Younger children can have this done for them in advance.) When opened up, the children should have a strip of seven figures. They then think of one kind thing they could do every day for a week for a member of their family or a friend, and write this down (or have it written down for them, or draw a little illustration) on each of the seven figures.

The kind deeds should be things that the children can realistically achieve during the coming week. If they can be encouraged to tick each 'good deed' off when it's been done, and bring their paper-people strip in the following week, saying a bit about how they got on, so much the better!

THE SENSE OF SOUND

WHAT CAN YOU HEAR?

When the visitor made his journey to his friend's home, he would have been surrounded by darkness and night-time noises. Some of the noises would have been familiar, but some might have been scary (wild animals, for instance). Even familiar noises, at night, can seem strange and frightening. Have any of the children been out very late, and noticed how sounds seem much louder at night than during the day? Why do they think that is? During the day-time there are a lot more noises around us than we usually realize, but because we're so busy doing other things, we don't really notice.

This activity is designed to help the children to be more aware of daytime sounds.

Get the children to sit on the floor, with as much space between them as possible, then close their eyes for a minute or two and listen very carefully. If any windows can be opened, so much the better. As they hear things, they can call them out, so that a list can be made. The children will probably be surprised to find just how much they have heard!

WHAT'S THE SOUND?

Although we use our sense of hearing a lot, we often don't use it very well because we rely on our sight so much more. If we couldn't see, our sense of hearing would become much better. But for most of us, when we can't see things, we find it difficult to recognize even quite familiar sounds.

> *You will need any of the items listed in the 'Let's hear it for the farmer!' activity on page 85, plus such things as a child's rattle, saucepan lids, coconut shells, wind-up toy, and so on.*

You can also include stamping your feet, clapping your hands, clicking your tongue, and so on, in this activity.

Stand so that the children have their backs to you, and then make the various sounds, one by one. The children can put up their hands and call out what they think each sound is—which won't be as easy as they expect! Walk round to the front of the children after each sound has been made, to show them what they actually heard.

THE SENSE OF TOUCH

WHAT IS IT?

There was no electricity in Jesus' day, and candles and oil-lamps didn't give out a great deal of light indoors by comparison. Outside, at night, unless there was a full moon, it wouldn't have been easy to see things, so people's sense of touch was probably much better than ours today, because they'd have had to rely on it far more. So, when some food was eventually handed over, the person receiving it quite probably stuck his hand in the basket to feel what was inside.

> *You will need some or all of the following items (some of which were used for the 'Have you got what I need?' activity on page 101), placed in a covered basket or box: a bread roll, small packet of cheese biscuits, packet of peanuts, packet of crisps, a potato, a hard-boiled egg, a plastic bottle of drink, a plastic bottle of ketchup, a carrot, a banana, a large mushroom, an apple, a lemon, a grapefruit, an orange, a pear.*

The children all sit with their backs to the box, then one volunteer at a time goes up to the box, reaches into the basket or box, and feels one item under the cover.

Using only their sense of touch, they must describe the item to the others to discover how quickly the other children can say what it actually is.

GOOD THINGS

God only gives us good things that we really need. We should do the same for each other.

> *You will need:*
> - *Two black plastic bags, each containing a T-shirt, coat, scarf, hat, gloves and pair of sunglasses.*
> - *Also in each bag, duplicate the clothing with items which feel very similar but don't look so good (for example, tights, gardening gloves, broken or garish sunglasses, dreadful-looking hats, granny's old coat, and so on).*
> - *Two blindfolds.*

Divide the children into two teams, then choose one child from each team who will be standing away from the others and blindfolded. Beside each blindfolded child should be placed one of the bags.

Each blindfolded child, or one of the leaders, should call out to their team one item at a time (starting with the T-shirt). Each team member must run up to the bag, *feel* for the item required (they must *not* look!) and then put it on the blindfolded child as quickly as they can. They then run to the back of their team as the next item is called out. When one of each of the items has been

put on each blindfolded team member, the blindfold is taken off so that they can see what they look like. The results might not be everything they really wanted!

THE SENSE OF SMELL

THE SMELL OF A STORY

If we could travel back to Jesus' day, we'd notice how different (and how much stronger) the smells were. If Jesus were describing these events today, the smells would be very different.

> *You will need some or all of the following items (empty containers would be fine): soap, shower gel, shampoo, bubble bath, deodorant, perfume, talcum powder, toothpaste, air freshener spray, cleaning fluid (non-toxic), disinfectant, washing powder and so on.*

The children should each sit with one of the above items just within reach.

Read the story below, pausing at any 'smelly' references. The children should raise 'their' item if they think it could be used to make that particular smell better!

It's midnight, and your time machine has landed you *plop!* inside the lower room of a family's small house in ancient Jerusalem. In the dimness you can just make out two sheep, three goats and a donkey—all snoring loudly and smelling dreadful,

because no one's changed the old, soiled hay for at least a month! You notice some steps, and climb up on to a raised area, where no fewer than fifteen people are crammed, sleeping on thin, wool-filled mattresses on a not-very-clean stone floor. There's a strong smell here, too, because water is very scarce, and so no one washes much. In the morning they'll rub some oil and home-made perfume into their skin, which might help. They could also use toothpaste, made from powdered oyster shells and honey, but that's far too expensive for this family. More smells come from the pile of outer clothes in the corner—only occasionally washed in the local river.

You clamber back past the animals to the front door. Maybe the air's fresher outside. But, no! In the middle of the square of houses are more animals and lots of chickens, huddled together, and the still air hangs heavily with the smell of food, cooked on open fires outside each house. Rotting in a corner is a pile of old vegetables and scraps of meat thrown to the animals earlier in the day, the remains of which have turned bad in the heat.

But it's time to go back to the 21st century now, so you clamber back into your time machine, and notice that it smells of… well, almost nothing at all!

SMELLS GREAT?

Spices and herbs which are familiar to us would also have been very familiar to Jesus—some as flavourings in food, but also (and probably even more so) as medicines and ointments.

> *You will need a selection of the following: cumin, dill, ginger, garlic, coriander, saffron, nutmeg, turmeric, cinnamon, and finely chopped herbs such as marjoram, oregano, rosemary, thyme, sage, mint and chives.*

Put a little of each on to saucers. (Mix with water, where necessary, to make a paste.) Number the saucers, with a corresponding list of contents for your own reference.

Let the children pass the saucers around, seeing if they can say what the smells are, or, more likely, what they remind them of—perhaps a curry dish, apple pies, toothpaste, stuffing from the turkey at Christmas, and so on.

THE SENSE OF TASTE

FOOD FOR A VISITOR

The visitor in this parable would have been happy to eat whatever was offered. He wouldn't have expected to have any choice. Today, though, we have lots of different choices, and like to know exactly what we're eating. It has to *look* OK, or we'll probably refuse to touch it! But what if we can't *see*? We'd still have to eat, but would we know what it was we were eating?

> *You will need:*
> - *A selection of different-flavoured biscuits, broken up into small pieces and put on plates, each plate labelled with its particular flavour.*
> - *Paper and pencils.*
> - *Blindfolds for half the number of children.*

Divide the children into pairs. One in each pair is blindfolded, and is 'the visitor'. Pair by pair, they move along the table. The visitor is given by their 'host' a little bit of biscuit to taste, and tries to guess what the flavour is (their partner mustn't help). The host gives the visitor a point for each flavour guessed correctly. (With younger children, the leaders can help with this.)

When the pairs get to the end of the row, the children swap places and the plates are moved into a different order. The activity is repeated until everyone has had a go (or the biscuits are finished). At the end, the children can check their lists to see how many guessed the right flavours.

TASTES GOOD?

Some of the more simple food we eat would have been very familiar to Jesus. A lot of our herbs and spices would have been known to him, and found in the homes of the people he spoke to. Can we recognize them just from the taste?

> *You will need:*
> - *Some or all of the items listed in the 'Smells great?' activity on page 104, mixed with cream cheese or mayonnaise, so that they're nicer to taste, and put on numbered saucers.*
> - *Several teaspoons.*
> - *A list to remind leaders what each flavour is.*

Children can volunteer for this activity, and choose which taste to risk trying. Can they guess the flavour? Does the taste remind them of any particular food? Does the taste match the smell?

STEP INTO REFLECTION

Have a flipchart, or similar, so that the children's ideas can be written up and easily seen.

Jesus told the parable about the friend arriving at midnight to help us to understand that God will always—and only—give us good things. But God doesn't give us everything we ask for, as soon as we ask for it, even if we ask lots and lots of times.

Older children can think about asking God to stop wars, prevent illnesses, make seriously ill people better, not let earthquakes or tornadoes happen, and so on.

Younger children can think about asking him to make sure they get everything they've asked for on their birthday, or not letting their pet rabbit die, and so on.

Invite the children to put up their hands if they think God ought to give us the things we ask for. Probably most of the children have, by now, got their hands up! Those who haven't can say why, and their answers can be noted on the flipchart. Make similar notes of why the others thought God *should* give us what we ask for. (Have some answers to both questions ready in your mind, so that you can guide younger children, especially, towards appropriate ideas.)

Jesus was very concerned to let us know how much God loves us, but if God were to give everyone exactly what they wanted, when they wanted it (just because they asked), life would be very chaotic. The following sketch is a simple way of showing this.

Using the different 'props', one person could take the part of all four characters, or you can use different people for each part—but a separate person will need to play the narrator. Make a simple picture of the weather each person is asking for, which can be held up after their speech. (Children can help with this.)

1. *With a beach towel*: I'm going to sunbathe in the garden today. So, God, I want you to make it really hot. Non-stop endless sunshine, please!
2. *Wearing a sun hat*: My old gran's coming for a visit today, but she burns very easily in the sun, so please, God, make it dry but cloudy for her, then she can sit out in our nice garden. Oh, and no wind! She absolutely hates the wind.
3. *Wearing an old jacket*: I'm a farmer, and I've just planted ten acres of wheat. What I need today, God, is a lovely lot of rain!
4. *Holding some clothes pegs*: There, that's all the washing hung out to dry. What I want right now, God, is no rain but plenty of wind. Please!
5. *Narrator*: All these people live in the same town. It would be ridiculous to try to give them all exactly what they want, don't you think…?

Invite the children to think again whether it would really work for God to give us all exactly what we want—even if what we're asking for is something good, like a nice day so that our gran can sit out in the garden, or something we truly need, like the farmer asking for rain for his newly planted crop.

Add their answers to the flipchart.

STEP INTO PRAYER

This prayer could be illustrated as suggested, and acted out, using:

- Outlines of trees from page 66.
- Outline of sheep from page 93, plus smaller outlines for the lamb, mane and long tail for the lion, pointed nose for the wolf, and so on.
- Weather illustrations.
- A string puppet and a robot toy, if available.

During the first two verses, the appropriate cards or sheets of illustrations can be shared out to the various children, so that they can hold them up.

In the fifth verse, one child (or a leader) takes most of the cards, and a couple of other children (or leaders) take the remaining few—thus leaving everyone else with nothing.

As the prayer comes to an end, the cards can be shared out again among all the others.

When God first made the world
he made it absolutely perfect.
The trees grew strong and tall
with lots of juicy fruit, all year round.
Quite the rosiest red apples you've ever seen!
The lions played with the little lambs.
The sheep and the wolf
were the best of friends.
The cats didn't chase the birds.
And the dogs didn't chase the cats.

The sun shone, but not too brightly.
In fact, the weather was just perfect.
Never too hot. Never too cold.
Never too dry. Never too wet.
Never too windy. Never too still.

And the people had everything they needed.
Just enough. Not too much.
God looked at it all, and knew
that it was great!

But then one day someone said,
'I want more!'
And another one said, 'I want more, too!'
And the snake said, 'Grab what you want.
Why shouldn't you?'

So they did.
Until some people had much, much more
than they needed.
And others had much, much less
than they needed.
While others had nothing at all.
And God looked at the world,
and felt very sad.

Then he had to decide just what
he should do.
Well, he didn't want us to be puppets,
so he didn't give us strings,
and he didn't want us to be robots,
so he didn't give us on/off switches.
He knew he just had to let us be free
to choose to care for one another
like he cares for us.
And, when we do that, he looks at us
and knows that we're just great!

Chapter 14

STEP INTO THE STORY OF GOD'S FAMILY

THE PARABLE OF THE WORKERS IN THE VINEYARD

MATTHEW 20:1–16

OLD TESTAMENT LINK

Everyone receives the full blessing of God's kingdom.

The 'Race with a difference' activity on page 110, set up beforehand, would make a good introduction to this parable.

What will happen to us when our lives are over? Whom does God choose to be with him in heaven? These are pretty big and important questions that we don't think about very often. *(Ask the children for their ideas. They're bound to have a few!)* Jesus was often asked, 'What do I have to *do* to get into heaven? Does God choose only certain, special people? And what will it be like?' They were difficult questions to answer but Jesus wanted us all to understand a little of the amazing mystery of the kingdom of heaven, so he told this parable.

There was once a man who owned a large vineyard —fields full of grapes growing in the sun, which would be made into wine. It was harvest time. The grapes were big, juicy and exactly ripe enough for picking. It would take a lot of workers, but though it was very early in the morning there were already people out looking for work. The usual rate of pay for a day's work was agreed, and those people went into the vineyard to make a start.

Later that morning (about 9am), realizing that he needed more workers, the vineyard owner went into the market-place and, seeing people hanging around with nothing to do, offered to pay them 'what was fair' if they would work for him that day. They happily agreed.

Even later (about noon), and again at about three o'clock, he returned to the market and each time made the same arrangement with others who were lazing around in the sunshine. But still he needed more (there were an awful lot of grapes!) so at about five in the afternoon, finding more people doing nothing because, they said, no one had yet hired them, he hired them to join the others in the vineyard.

Finally, with all the grapes picked, the workers went to collect their money. And now something unusual happened. The manager was told by the vineyard owner to pay the people *first* who'd arrived *last*. Not only that, but he was told to pay them a full day's wage—for just one hour's work! Now, the people who'd worked the longest thought that meant they'd get even more money, but when it came to their turn they got the same amount, and they didn't like that one little bit! So they complained—loudly!

'Those people have only worked for an hour,' they protested, 'but you've given them the same money as us and we've worked in the hot sun all day long! It's not fair!'

'I haven't cheated you,' pointed out the owner. 'We agreed what you'd be paid at the start of the day, and you were quite happy with the amount. It's my money and if I choose to pay everyone the same because I'm a generous man, that's my business, not yours!'

Jesus wants us to know that God is just the same! Being the first, or the best, or working the hardest or the longest during our lives doesn't actually impress God. He cares just as much for those who come last, but do as much as they can. During our lives, as well as after them, he is there for absolutely *everyone*, and will always be far more generous to each one of us than we human beings are able (or willing) to be to each other.

Like the workers in the vineyard, we might want to say, 'That's not fair! I deserve much more than them!' But if he's being extra generous to *you*, you probably wouldn't complain!

STEP INTO THE SENSES

THE SENSE OF SIGHT

A RACE WITH A DIFFERENCE!

This activity will be far more effective if it's done before telling the parable.

Create a start and finish line, marking it with chairs. Line the children up on the start line. On the word 'Go!' they must run to the finish line. Ask the children who they think won. They will of course point to the one who crossed the line first. Now ask who came last. It's likely that the winner is the tallest and strongest in the group, and will be feeling pleased with themselves, while the loser is the smallest and slightest, and won't!

Now explain that, actually, the one who came in last is the first—the 'winner'—and the first now becomes the last. This will, inevitably, deflate the 'winner' but please the 'loser', but explain that this was a race run with God's much kinder, more generous rules, which certainly don't always match ours!

Jesus said that 'everyone who is now first will be last, and everyone who is last will be first'. That sounds like a very topsy-turvy way of looking at things, but Jesus often wanted people to see their lives, and the world, in a totally new way.

MAKE A SHADOW CLOCK

Wrist-watches hadn't been invented at the time of Jesus, so how was the vineyard owner able to tell what time he hired the workers? Actually, in a sunny country like Israel, it was quite easy. You just looked at where the sun was and how long the shadows were. The children can do exactly the same thing now with the help of a shadow clock.

> *You will need one cotton reel and two pencils per child, a square of card or plain paper for each child, and glue.*

Glue the cotton reel into the centre of each square of card. Put a blob of glue on to the blunt end of one pencil, and push it into the hole in the cotton reel, so that it sticks to the paper in an upright position. If it's sunny outside, the children can immediately discover where the shadow of the reel and pencil lies on the card, drawing around the shadow and putting the time beside it.

By drawing around the shadows at different times of the day, they'll discover which times make the longest and shortest shadows on their home-made clocks. They can also look at the length of other shadows outside, and make a note of the time and length of the shadows. Then, when they next see similar-length shadows, they'll be able to amaze their friends by knowing very closely what time of day it is, even if they don't have a watch!

THE SENSE OF SOUND

TIME FOR A JOB

As we know, the workers in Jesus' parable were hired at different times of the day—early (probably around 6am), then 9am, noon, 3pm and 5pm. This activity will help the children to remember the times and so, too, the rest of the parable.

> *You will need a bell, spoon, fork and plate, and the five times of the day, brightly written on sheets of paper.*

Place the time-sheets on the walls around the room, in any sort of order. Use different sounds for the different times of the day. For example:

6am: 'Cock-a-doodle-do!'
9am: Ring a bell.
Noon: Clatter cutlery on a plate.
3pm: 'Yawn! Yawn! Time for a break!'
5pm: 'Slurp! Slurp! Time for tea!'

The children start off standing in the middle of the room, then run as quickly as they can to the correct 'time' place when the relevant sound is made. If there's a large number of children, the last one to reach the right place can be declared 'out'. With a smaller number they can just enjoy trying to get there first.

GOD IS FOR EVERYONE!

Jesus wants us know that God cares about everyone, not just those who work the hardest or longest, or never make mistakes (nothing wrong with all that, of course—just that it doesn't make us especially perfect). And he's not there only for those born in a certain part of the world, either.

God will welcome you as his own special child whoever you are, whatever you do, however you look, and whichever language you speak. He will always listen to you.

But how good are *we* at listening to each other? Often it feels as though we're each speaking a different language! Write some simple foreign phrases on paper. For example:

'We are friends':	a. Nous sommes amis
	b. Wij zijn friends
	c. Siame amici
'You are special':	a. Vous êtes special
	b. U bent special
	c. Sei spéciale
'God loves us':	a. Dieu nous aime
	b. God hou onze
	c. Dio ci ama

Hand the sheets to half the number of children in the group, quietly giving them some idea of the pronunciation (total accuracy is not a requirement). They then sit on a row of chairs in the middle of the room.

Whisper one phrase each to the remaining children (note who has which phrase). Those children then walk around the row of chairs, as the seated children repeat their phrases, trying to find the phrase that you whispered to them. When they think they've found the right phrase, both children go to the leader who has the list to see if they've successfully heard and recognized their partner.

THE SENSE OF TOUCH

THE FEEL OF MONEY

The amount of money agreed for a full day's work in the vineyard was probably one single coin—the silver Roman 'denarius'. The workers who'd done only an hour's work might have expected, instead, to get a bronze Roman 'as', because that was worth about ten times less than a denarius. Or perhaps a few Greek 'leptons'—it took 128 of those to be worth the same as one denarius. Or they could all have been paid using the local Jewish money. That sounds very confusing—and probably was! It would be like us shopping with a mixture of English, American and Japanese coins in our pockets. If you were a blind person in Jesus' day, your sense of touch would have been especially important to help you tell one kind of coin from another.

How well can the children's sense of touch help them choose the right coins?

> *You will need: 1p, 5p, 10p, 20p, 50p and £1 coins (if toy money is available, all the better), and paper bags or small envelopes, each containing, preferably, one of each value of coin.*

Put the bags out on a table. Then, choosing the same number of children, ask them each to go to a bag and, using only their sense of touch, to find a certain

coin. When they think they've found it (or you think they've had long enough!) they should hold it up. How many have managed to find the right coin? Repeat until all the children have had at least one go.

HEAVEN AND EARTH

Jesus tried to explain at other times, as well as in this parable, a little of what heaven will be like, and just how different it will be from life here on earth. Although it's still impossible for us really to imagine exactly what heaven (being with God) will be like, we can be sure it'll be the most beautiful of places, and full of only good things.

Make a very effective banner with rough things for 'earth', and soft for 'heaven'.

> *You will need a length of plain wallpaper, with a thick dividing line down the middle for heaven and earth, plenty of glue, and sticky tape.*
> - *For heaven: soft/furry material, silk/satin, ribbons, leather, suede, cotton wool, plastic, soft paper tissue, soft sponge, velvet, sequins, smooth and brightly coloured cardboard, plastic pop-wrap, smooth, shiny paper, and so on.*
> - *For earth: rough towelling, scouring cloth, velcro, tinfoil, chopped straws, net curtaining, crepe paper, thick string, rough sponge, twigs, shells from nuts, screwed-up paper, polystyrene packaging, plastic bottle tops, seeds, dried beans, pasta, and so on.*

The children can *feel* the difference between each side—far better than just looking!

THE SENSE OF SMELL

THE SMELL OF A DAY

We don't know why those people, still at the market-place at five in the afternoon, hadn't been given work. Possibly they weren't considered worth employing because, perhaps, they couldn't see properly, or hear what was being said. But the vineyard owner in Jesus' parable wouldn't have let anything like that stop him from giving people a job. He'd have known they could still do valuable work.

If the children couldn't *see* the time, or how dark or light it was outside; couldn't *hear* any noises to help them judge what time of day it was; and weren't able to *ask* anyone because they couldn't speak, how would they know if it was time for breakfast, lunch or tea—or getting up, or going to bed, or going to the market-place to try to get work? What other sense could they use, apart from touch? Well, of course, there are still their *noses*!

You will need (on lightly covered, unbreakable dishes, all looking the same):
- *toothpaste (early morning)*
- *marmalade (9am)*
- *crisps (noon)*
- *chocolate biscuits (3pm)*
- *peanut butter/jam (5pm)*
- *soap (bedtime)*

You will also need sheets of paper with the above items brightly written on them, one on each sheet, perhaps adding a simple drawing of which item represents which time.

Fix the sheets of paper up around the room. Working with six children at a time, give them one of the dishes and tell them they have to decide what time of day it represents, *using only their sense of smell*. Then they have to go, with their dish, to the relevant 'time' around the room.

Discover how many got the smell right. Then, mixing the dishes around, give them to any remaining children until everyone's had a go.

SMELLS HEAVENLY!

God is generous enough to make heaven a brilliant place for all different kinds of people. It'll look great, and smell even better!

You will need magazines, travel brochures, mail-order books, and so on, cards for each child, plus smelly gel pens, soap or floral spray.

The children can cut out pictures of things/ scenes/places they'd like to find in heaven, if they had a choice, and stick them on to their card. Then make them smell nice, using the above items, to create a heavenly smelling card.

THE SENSE OF TASTE

TOPSY-TURVY FOOD

Jesus wanted to teach, through his parables, that God loves us much more than we can possibly realize, and wants to give us all much more than we even deserve. But this troubled a great many important leaders at the time, because what he said often turned their rules and regulations upside down, inside out and back to front!

To help them remember this, the children can make some topsy-turvy food!

You will need fizzy drink, ice-cream, thin white bread, sliced cheese or ham, icing sugar, milk, food colouring, savoury cream crackers.

Upside-down 'pudding'

Normally, you'd put ice-cream in a dish and then pour something over it to add to the flavour.

Instead, in half a glassful of any fizzy drink, put a dessertspoonful of ice-cream. It has an interesting effect, and tastes great, too!

Inside-out sandwiches

Trim the crusts off a slice of bread, then cut it into four pieces. Four children can then make themselves an inside-out sandwich, by putting each piece of bread between small slices of cheese or ham.

Back-to-front biscuits

Mix icing sugar with milk to make a thick paste. Add a little food colouring, then spread the paste between small cream crackers to make sweet-savoury biscuits.

GOD'S HANDS

You will need a wrapped sweet, or small chocolate bar, for each child.

Sit the children down in a circle and hand each one a sweet or chocolate bar. Tell each child very firmly they are *not* allowed to eat that particular sweet, but that, of course, you do want them to have a sweet. If they're beginning to get the message, they'll quickly realize that they need to give their own sweet away—although the risk is that they won't necessarily receive a sweet back from anyone. Hopefully, though, everyone will decide to be generous so that everyone gets a sweet to eat!

God is wonderfully kind and generous but he needs *us* to do some of that good stuff for him. We need to be God's arms and legs, eyes and ears, feet and hands. That's why it pleases God when we're thoughtful and generous towards each other, because then we're being more like him—more like he created us to be.

STEP INTO REFLECTION

We know that the people who'd started work at the vineyard last were paid first. Then, after telling this parable, Jesus added, 'Everyone who is now first will be last, and everyone who is last will be first.'

Do the children think that sounds unfair—especially when the parable also says that God is very generous? It's certainly not the way *we* do things!

After all, how would we feel if this happened to us?

You've gone to a theme park, and are waiting at the front of a long queue for your turn to ride on a brilliant giant rollercoaster. Finally, the cars speed down the slope and stop. It's your turn at last, but—hang on a minute!—God's suddenly taken charge, and is letting the ones at the back of the queue get on first, while you have to wait right until the last! That's *certainly* not fair!

Well, going by our 'rules', it isn't, and probably all the children will agree! But now try the following (you'll need a bag full of sweets for this).

Hold up the bag of sweets, then ask the children to form a line in front of you quickly so that you can give them one each.

It's very likely that the children who are bigger, more confident, or just quicker on their feet, will get to the front first, assuming that you'll start at the front of the queue. If this happens, start with the last in the queue, giving them a sweet first—because these sweets are being given out the way Jesus would do it, so the last comes first.

(However, be prepared for the children to realize that, this time, the first won't always come first. They might decide that being last in the queue would be better! But what were their real motives for doing that? Who should get the sweets first now?)

The special message here is that we need to do things God's way, and take particular care of those who are not able to put themselves first. Being strong, capable, clever, rich or famous might make us seem more important to other human beings, but God never measures us by such things. Thank goodness he doesn't!

Now give the children another sweet, but this time in reverse order—because those who were given one *first* before should now come *last*.

Those are God's rules. Perfectly fair, for everyone, every time!

STEP INTO PRAYER

Since God turns our 'rules' back to front, upside down and inside out, perhaps he likes topsy-turvy prayers as well! Here's one.

It would be good if this could be printed out so that each child can take a copy away with them. They could make a topsy-turvy illustration to go with it.

Perhaps the children could make up a verse or two for themselves.

They could also make very simple, large illustrations of a couple of the verses, and use them to accompany saying the prayer in church, adding actions and so on to give the adults an idea of what they've been learning about.

Wouldn't it be great
if the rain rained up
and the sun rolled about on the ground?
If the snow turned green
and the wind could be seen,
while the moon turned his smile to a frown!

Wouldn't it be cool
if we walked on our hands,
with our feet floating up in the air?
We'd have shoes on our fingers,
and hats on our toes,
and our ankles would grow lots of hair!

Wouldn't it be fun
if the thing that was done
was to help everybody in need.
Imagine us all being friends—
never arguing again—
and God's love in the world being freed.

Wasn't it just wild
that God sent his child
to be the Saviour of everyone here?
He was weak, but so strong.
Never did one thing wrong.
We can't see him, but he's always near.

Yes, wouldn't it be strange
if all our rules were changed?
Topsy-turvy: from death until birth!
If we do things God's way,
starting right now—today—
We'll see glimpses of heaven—on earth!

Chapter 15

STEP INTO THE STORY OF GOD'S BLESSINGS

THE PARABLE OF THE WATCHFUL/FAITHFUL SERVANT

LUKE 12:35–48

OLD TESTAMENT LINK

God rewards faithfulness with the blessings of his kingdom.

Oh no! It's one of those days! Old Aunt Mildred is coming to visit. She hasn't been for ages, but you still remember how, last time, she turned up unexpectedly, and you had to sit still on the sofa for hours 'like a good child'. You hardly dared breathe, let alone squirm or scratch your nose! She frowned at all the toys scattered over the floor, tutted loudly at every bit of dust she made quite sure she found, and turned up her nose at any food that came out of a packet. So this time Mum's gone mad all morning, baking cakes that you know you won't get to eat 'cos Aunt Mildred'll scoff the lot, and cleaning and tidying everything in the house hours earlier than necessary, to make sure it'll all be ready (so you'll be in *big* trouble if you mess anything up). Even worse, Mum makes *you* get all clean and smart ages before you think you really need to, because she says Aunt Mildred didn't say exactly what time she'd arrive, and she wants you to be ready, too.

Well, this next parable is all about being ready. Jesus told it to remind us that we don't actually *know* what's going to happen to us next year, or next week—or even in this next hour, so we need to be prepared for anything. He also wanted to say that, if we stay faithful to God, being ready to do what he asks, he'll reward us with many unexpected blessings.

'So be ready,' Jesus said, 'and keep your lamps burning, just like servants ought to do when they are waiting for their master to come home from a wedding feast.'

The servants in this story didn't know whether their master would get back late at night from the wedding feast, or early in the morning, but they *did* know they ought to be awake and ready to give him whatever he wanted once he got home. It can't have been easy to stay awake but Jesus said that, when their master knocked, those who were always ready to open the door for him—no matter what the time—were very fortunate. They would find him so pleased with them, he'd make them sit down and wait on *them* for a change! Then Jesus must have smiled. After all, he said, no one would let a thief break into their home if they had any idea that a robbery was planned, would they? No, of course not. They'd be awake—ready and waiting! So always be ready, Jesus said, because, in the same way, you don't know when the Son of Man will come. (And you certainly want to be ready for *him*.)

Now the disciple, Peter, who was with Jesus at the time, asked him to explain more. So Jesus said that servants who are always faithful will be put in charge of everything the master owns. But suppose there's a servant who thinks his master won't get back till very late. Great! Now he can eat and drink as much as he wants of his master's food and wine, and be really cruel to the rest of the servants. But then, suddenly, there his master is—home much earlier than expected. The servant isn't ready for him at all! The master is very angry to find his servant behaving so badly. He punishes him and throws him out of the house, because he can't be trusted.

But Jesus then added that, if the man hadn't actually *known* what his master wanted him to do, he wouldn't have been punished quite so badly.

Jesus also said that if God has given you good things, he will expect you to do good things in return. And the more generous God is to you, the better and kinder and more generous you have to be towards other people—which is only fair, don't you think?

STEP INTO THE SENSES

THE SENSE OF SIGHT

CHANGING FACES

There would have been times when the master was pleased with his servants, and other times, as in the parable, when he would have been very disappointed and angry. Our lives will be much better if we always try to make God happy. But sometimes, unfortunately, we get things wrong, and make him sad instead. Fortunately for us, he's also very forgiving, and ready to smile at us again.

You will need A4 cards folded in half, 15cm diameter circles of cardboard and split-pin paper-fasteners (enough for one per child), plus pens, pencils and crayons.

Cut two slots, both 6cm wide x 2.5cm deep, in the front of each card. One should be 5cm from the top, and the other 5cm from the bottom. Both should be 2.5cm in from the fold. Using the paper-fastener, fix the circle of cardboard behind the front of the card, 1cm to the right of centre (away from the fold), so that the circle sticks out a little on the right side of the card, and can thus be easily turned. In the two 'windows' on the front of the card, the children can draw angry-looking eyes at the top, and an angry mouth at the bottom. Turn the circular card so that those drawings disappear and, in the now clear 'windows', they can draw happy-looking eyes and mouth. The rest of the face can be drawn on the front of the card, with the head of the paper-fastener forming part of the nose!

CAN YOU GUESS?

Good servants not only had to be ready at all times for their master's arrival, but often had to think about what he might need or want, even before he asked for it. That can't always have been very easy! How good are the children at doing it?

You will need:
* *A box full of a few different objects—for example, torch, notepad, clock, book, pen, sunglasses, magazine, comb, brush, news-paper, and so on.*
* *A bag with pieces of paper or card, with one of the above items written on each. (For younger children, a simple illustration should be added.)*

One child (the 'master') chooses a piece of paper or card from the bag. Another child (a 'servant') picks an item out of the box and holds it up. Then the 'master' holds up their card. Has the servant guessed correctly what the master wanted? If they have, they're a very good servant, and should receive a reward! Continue as many times as required.

THE SENSE OF SOUND

WHO'S THERE?

Jesus spoke about some very serious things, but he also had a great sense of fun. When he talked about 'being ready', he also joked that, if you knew exactly when a thief was going to break into your home, you'd try to be ready to stop him. In fact, you'd try to be ready to stop him even if you didn't know when he was coming. Jesus also wants us to be ready when he himself comes to make changes in our lives. But we have to listen well, so that we know what God wants us to do!

You will need to:
a. *use something to make a knocking sound (for the master).*
b. *use a metal tray and cutlery to make a clattering noise (for the thief).*
c. *ring a bell (for a visitor).*
d. *clap your hands (for Jesus and God).*

Make sure the children can't see what you're doing, but have to rely on hearing the sounds. For each of the different sounds, they do the following:

Sound a. Stand to attention for the master.
Sound b. Crouch, ready to pounce on the thief.
Sound c. Tidy hair and clothes, ready for the visitor.
Sound d. Kneel down, with hands outstretched and palms upwards, ready to receive God's blessings.

NB. In this activity, no one should be 'out' for getting the actions wrong. It can simply be repeated several times, getting quicker to make it more fun.

ARE YOU REALLY LISTENING?

Below is an alternative version of the parable, with some deliberate mistakes. If the children think they've heard something wrong they should stand up quickly and say, 'Stop! That's not right!' The first to call out should say what they think is the 'correct' version. If they don't get it right, ask another child. The emphasis should be on helping them to listen and have fun, rather than trying to catch out their own mistakes.

Be ready, and keep your lamps low, just like those servants who put their feet up and wait for their master to return from his holiday. As soon as they hear his key in the lock, they know they can go to bed. Servants are fortunate if their master finds them asleep when he arrives. He'll wake them up, sit them down and serve them. After all, you would certainly let a thief break into your home, wouldn't you, if you knew when he was coming?

A servant who is always faithful will, perhaps, be put in charge of one or two things. But suppose one of the servants thinks the master won't be home until late, so behaves very badly. If the master

arrives home unexpectedly early, and catches him eating his food, drinking his best wine, and being cruel to the other servants, he'll be very pleased with him and put him in charge of everything he owns. And servants who don't know what the master wants them to do will be punished worse than the others, if they get things wrong.

If God has been very generous to you, he will expect you to keep it all for yourself!

THE SENSE OF TOUCH

WHAT'S IN THE WAY?

The master wanted servants whom he could trust to take care of his precious belongings as well as he would himself. In the same way, God needs to be able to trust us to look after all his precious belongings—which include you, me, the world and the entire universe! But there are many things that get in the way and make it difficult to see what he wants us to do.

You will need one tray per child, holding a plastic flower pot, old spoon, soil/sand, a sturdy flower (real or plastic), a small container with a little water, plastic or gardening gloves, a blindfold.

While blindfolded, wearing the gloves and using the spoon, each child should put soil or sand into their pot, then plant their flower and water it. (Set a time limit.) When they've all finished, they can remove the blindfolds and see who's done the best job!

KEEP THOSE LAMPS BURNING!

In Jesus' day, with no electricity, it was vital in each home to keep one oil lamp burning, so that other lamps could be quickly lit from the one flame. It was an extremely important part of a servant's job to keep their own lamp burning, so that they'd always be ready to attend to their master's needs. They had to have fresh oil handy, and keep the wick in their lamp properly trimmed. Careless or lazy servants, who didn't bother, could find that their lamps had gone out just when they needed them most! No wonder Jesus compared 'keeping our lamps burning' to being always ready for God.

Today, Jesus might say that we should always have our torches handy! That sounds easy enough, but what if it's the middle of a very dark night, the electricity's gone off, your torch needs new batteries, and someone is knocking at the front door, needing help?

You will need one tray per team, holding a torch, batteries, a blindfold and pair of gloves.

Divide the children into small teams. Explain which way the batteries have to go in to the torches. The first in the team runs up to their tray, puts on the blindfold and gloves, puts the batteries in the torch and fixes the torch back together. They then remove the blindfold and gloves and turn the torch on. If their 'lamp' is 'burning', they get a point (and their team can give them a big cheer). They put all the items back on the tray and run to the back of their team, so that the next child can have a go, and so on.

If the team that finishes first *also* 'lit' the most torches, they are the winners. If not, the team that finished first competes with those who 'lit' the most torches. But it's the team of 'servants' that lights the most torches that finally wins!

NB: With younger children, you can omit the blindfold.

THE SENSE OF SMELL

USING YOUR NOSES

Because most of us rely on our eyes so much, we often don't notice the job that our noses do! Dogs are amazing at being able to pick people out of a crowd, just from their smell (good smells—not just nasty smells). If the servants had been as clever, they could have smelt their master arriving home, even as he walked past an open window.

> *You will need perfumed sprays.*

One of the leaders should decide which smell will be the 'master's'. Making sure the children can't tell which spray they're being given, lightly spray

the right-hand wrist of just one child with the 'master's' spray, and all of the rest of the children with one of the other sprays. The children should hold up their own 'smelly' wrists and check everyone else's to try to decide who has a different smell, and thus is the 'master'. When they've made their choice, they should follow the 'master' around, until everyone has finished choosing.

This can be repeated using other sprays (applied to the other wrist and backs of hands).

NB: Tell the children beforehand that even when/if they realize they are the master, they can pretend to choose someone else—and put the others off the scent!

WHAT HAVE YOU BEEN DOING?

The servant who behaved badly thought that he could get away with anything because his master wasn't around to see. He forgot that God knows exactly what we're doing, all the time. Often we think that if there's no one around to see, we can do all sorts of naughty things. If Mum can't *see* us take those chocolates out of the box, she won't know. But, somehow, she always does! Maybe it's the *smell* of the chocolate that does it!

> *You will need plain paper bags, each containing a dry food product, such as coconut, tea leaves, coffee powder, mint leaves, curry powder, ginger, crushed crisps in varying flavours, and so on, plus one more plain bag containing grated chocolate.*

This time, the leaders are the servants, and the children, collectively, are the 'master'. The children turn their backs on the servants, who are pretending to prepare the master's evening meal by putting their hands in the paper bags, thus getting different food smells on their fingers. However, one of the 'servants' leaves the cooking to everyone else and dips his or her fingers into the master's private chocolate box, instead. Can the children, by using their sense of smell, pick out the culprit?

THE SENSE OF TASTE

LET'S BE GENEROUS!

> *You will need some fairly plain biscuits, broken into bite-sized pieces, plus similar pieces of chocolate-covered biscuits. You will also need four plates. Set aside some unbroken chocolate biscuits.*

Lay the pieces of plain biscuit flat on the plates, adding to each plate one clearly visible piece of chocolate biscuit. Lightly cover the plates and put them on a table. (Each plate should hold one more piece of biscuit than the total number of children.)

One at a time, the children should go to the table, take one piece of biscuit from the first plate, and eat it (without letting anyone else see what they've taken). Repeat for each plate, but get the children to go up in a different order each time.

Then ask the children what sorts of biscuits were on the plates. If the chocolate biscuits were eaten first, most of the children won't even know there were any chocolate ones! But if they've got the message about being generous, all four chocolate biscuit pieces will be left on the plates (for the leaders!).

Jesus asks us to be generous and thoughtful towards each other. So the children should get a whole chocolate biscuit each, anyway, to show how generous everyone ought to be.

WHAT WILL YOU GET?

Servants who were always willing and ready would often be rewarded by their master. If we trust God enough to put our lives in his hands, we'll be rewarded, too, in many unexpected ways. We can't choose the reward, but God only gives us good things, so the reward will always be nice. We just have to learn to trust him.

You will need some, or all, of the following, in separate plastic containers:
- *Frankfurter sausages, sliced.*
- *Mild cheese, chopped into small pieces.*
- *Halved grapes / small pieces of apple and pear / small bits of tinned fruit.*
- *Small pieces of carrot / celery / cucumber / tomato.*
- *Plenty of plastic dessert spoons and paper serviettes.*

Let the children choose a partner. (Make one group of three if there's an odd number.) Invite all of them to take a spoon and select three of their favourite pieces of food from any of the containers, then cover the spoon lightly with a serviette.

When everyone's done that, tell them to get back into their pairs, facing each other. Now they're going to eat what's on the spoon—except that it'll be the other person's spoon. One at a time, one child closes their eyes while the other uncovers their spoon and pops the food they've chosen into their partner's mouth. Will they trust each other that they've each made a nice choice? Can they also say what was on the spoon? Repeat as required.

STEP INTO REFLECTION

Remember 'Aunt Mildred'—the one we were supposed to be ready for? She didn't sound very friendly, or kind, or generous, did she? So why did Mum make a big effort to make sure she'd feel welcome and comfortable, and have things ready to eat that she'd really like?

Was that a silly thing to do, and a waste of time? Or was it kind and thoughtful? Should we expect other people to fit in with us (so we don't have to change anything for them)? Would old Aunt Mildred, maybe, have been a bit nicer when she saw that we'd gone to some trouble to make her happy?

It's often difficult to see things from other people's point of view, so the children can look at it from their own point of view! Read them the following story, and then see what they think.

You've made a new friend at school, and have arranged to go to tea. But you haven't been in their house long before things begin to look bad! First of all, your friend shows you their brilliant new computer games, but won't let you play any of them. You sit for an hour getting bored, only being allowed to watch *them* play. And you're told not to touch anything else. (Everything in the house is kept horribly tidy—and that includes your friend's bedroom. You hardly dare move.)

Now at last, though, you've been called down-stairs for tea. This should be OK because, when you arrived, your friend's mum had asked if there was anything you don't like eating. You said you don't eat beefburgers, don't like chips or cooked fruit, and custard makes you feel sick. So what have you got? Oh no! Beefburgers, peas and chips, followed by baked apple and custard! And it's quickly clear that you're expected to eat everything on your plate because the family doesn't like to see anything being wasted. All this makes you feel really fed up, grumpy and miserable. You hardly speak to your so-called friend, and you'll *never, ever* go to their house again!

- How much better would it have been if your friend's mum had given you things to eat that she knew you'd like?
- And if your friend had shared their brand new computer games with you, even if you couldn't do them as well?
- What if you'd been allowed to play with something else in the room? Would it have been a waste of your friend's time to have to clear things up afterwards?
- How would you have felt when you discovered that your friend didn't want to have to change anything they usually did, even though you were there?
- Would you have been nicer to everyone if they'd gone to any trouble to make you happy?

Because we are all God's children, and part of his family, we should do what God wants.

And what does God want? That's easy! He wants us all to have a good and happy life. And how do we do that? That's easy, too! We should treat other people in exactly the same way we'd like to be treated—no matter who they are.

STEP INTO PRAYER

A PRAYER TO SING

Sing this song to the tune of 'Ten Green Bottles'.

*There were five good servants
ready with their lamps.
Five good servants
staying wide awake.
But if one of those servants
should start to fall asleep,
there'll be four good servants
ready with their lamps.*

*Four good servants
keeping all things safe. (Repeat)
But if one of those servants
should break the master's rules,
there'll be three good servants
ready with their lamps.*

*Three good servants
always very kind. (Repeat)
But if one of those servants
should start to turn quite cruel,
there'll be two good servants
ready with their lamps.*

*Two good servants
in charge of food supplies. (Repeat)
But if one good servant
stole all the food himself
there'll be one good servant
ready with his lamp.*

*One good servant
that everyone could trust. (Repeat)
And with one good servant
to light the other's way,
there'll be lots of good servants
faithful to the end.*

STEP INTO THE STORY OF GOD'S NEW RULES

THE PARABLE OF THE GOOD SAMARITAN

LUKE 10:25–37

OLD TESTAMENT LINK

Love your neighbour as yourself.

This parable could be introduced by using the 'Help the traveller home!' activity on page 130.

'What do we have to do to have eternal life?' That was the big question Jesus was asked once by a clever man who knew a lot about the Law of Moses. So Jesus asked him what God had said to Moses. The man smiled. That was easy! 'We should love God with all our heart, soul, strength and mind, and then love our neighbour as much as we love ourselves,' he replied. 'Well done!' Jesus said. 'And that's how to get eternal life.'

'Yes, but, hang on a minute!' the man said. 'Just who are these "neighbours"?' Now Jesus could have given a very simple answer to that one, but he knew that the man—and all of us—would remember a story much better, and this is one of his most famous.

There was a man, Jesus said, travelling along a narrow pass on the desolate mountain road leading from Jerusalem to Jericho. Unfortunately for the man, robbers suddenly appeared, beat him up, stole everything he had and left him to die under the hot, hot sun.

After a little while, a priest happened to be travelling the same route and saw the man lying in a heap at the side of the road. Did he stop and help the injured man? Well, no, actually, he didn't. 'He's no one I know,' he thought to himself, 'and if he's already dead, or dies while I'm taking care of him, I'll have to be purified before I can work in the temple again—and that takes seven days. It's far too inconvenient!' The priest, of course, said a prayer for the man, but stayed well over the other side of the road, and hurried on his way towards Jericho.

Some time later a man from the tribe of Levi—the people who did all the work around the temple—passed by. Did *he* stop to help the injured man? No, he didn't either. Just like the priest, he had the same fear about touching a dead body, but maybe he also thought the man could be a robber himself, just pretending to be injured. It might be a trick to rob him! 'Someone else is bound to come along soon,' he thought. 'They can take care of him.'

And he was quite right, because a couple of hours later, a man from Samaria came riding his donkey down the road. However, if either the priest or the Levite had seen him, they'd have immediately declared, 'Huh! A Samaritan. They've been our enemies for centuries. That man'll get no help from a dreadful person like that!'

But, do you know, they'd have been quite wrong, because the Samaritan immediately stopped and hurried over to the man. The Samaritan didn't know who he was, but he immediately began to wash his wounds with olive oil and wine (often used as ointments and medicine), then tore up some of his own clothing for bandages. Then he put him carefully on his donkey and made the

long, hot journey to the nearest inn, continuing to care for the man through the night. The next morning the Samaritan gave the innkeeper two silver coins, and said, 'Please take care of this man. If you spend more than this on him, I'll pay you when I return this way.'

Then Jesus asked the clever man, 'Which of these three people was a real neighbour to the man beaten up by the robbers?' *(What do the children think?)* The man answered that it was the one who stopped to help. 'That's quite right,' Jesus said, 'so go and do the same thing!'

STEP INTO THE SENSES

THE SENSE OF SIGHT

WHAT CAN I DO FOR YOU?

Jesus told this parable because he wanted us to know that, as well as putting God first, the most important thing we can do with our lives is to help each other. The trouble is, we often don't want to be bothered, so we look for an excuse—any excuse.

You will need pens/pencils, strips of two different colours of paper or card (so that each child has one of each colour) and a cereal packet-sized cardboard box.

On one coloured piece of paper, the children should write down a helpful thing they could do for someone. On the other coloured piece, they should write an excuse not to do it. The strips should then be folded and dropped into the box. (Give them a good shake.) Now it's swap time! Each child should pick out two different coloured strips, and some can be read out. What do they think of the excuses that have been made? Some might sound silly, but we all often make unreasonable excuses for not doing things.

DO I KNOW YOU?

The traveller didn't recognize the Samaritan as a friend. But this unknown person proved himself to be a good friend. Once we get to know them, we'd always recognize our friends, wouldn't we? Or would we? The children can find out!

You will need:
- *Ready-made masks that are all exactly the same, or cardboard strips with eye cut-outs, and elastic or string for fixing. The masks can be put together beforehand, or the children can do it, but they should all look the same.*
- *Dressing-up items to create a quick disguise for each child. The children's own outdoor coats could be used, as long as they are swapped over so that no one wears their own coat, and scarves or towels could be used to hide their hair.*

Divide the children into Samaritans and travellers. The Samaritans go out of the room for a few moments while the travellers are quickly disguised and their masks put on. Sit the travellers down on chairs at the far end of the room. A few cries of

You will need:
- *Cut-off bases of plastic bottles (4 cm deep), with a very small hole in each base, two for every pair of children. (Alternatively, you could use plastic cups or clean yoghurt pots.)*
- *A ball of thin string.*

Working in pairs, the children should connect two of the bottle bases, threading a length of string through the holes in each and knotting securely on the inside. Standing so that the string is tightly stretched between them (with nothing touching it), the children should be able to hear each other speaking when one speaks into the 'phone' and the other holds it to their ear. Use the phones for the next activity.

'Help!' and 'Save me!' would be great, just as the others enter the room.

The Samaritans return to the room. As they enter, each one is quietly told which friend it is they've got to rescue. *(Make a note of who has been given which name.)* When they've all been given a name, the Samaritans make their choice from looking at the travellers' eyes, and lead their chosen child down to 'safety' at the other end of the room. When they've all chosen (and some will have wanted to choose the same child, but that's fine), the masks are removed. How many made the correct choice? The groups can then switch, to repeat the activity.

THE SENSE OF SOUND

LET'S COMMUNICATE!

If Jesus told this story today, he'd probably say that the man who was attacked phoned various friends for help on his mobile (it was last month's model, so the robbers didn't bother stealing it!), but only got their answerphones. The children can make their own 'phones' and, after that, send their individual 'help' messages.

DID YOU SAY 'HELP'?

Even when we're asked for help, we don't always understand what's being asked for, so we need to listen carefully.

You will need 'phones' made in the previous activity, and pens and paper for writing down the messages.

The children need to work out a message based on the letters of their own first names. The message can be as silly or sensible as they wish. For example, for Susan: 'Send Us Some Apples Now!' For Thomas: 'Take Home Our Matching African Sausages!'

To make it more difficult, older children can disguise their name in a slightly longer sentence—for example, 'Send us some apples now because we haven't eaten in days!'

Divide the children into two groups. Group 1 sit, each child holding one end of a phone and a message written on paper. The messages should have been muddled up, so that, if possible, no one has their own. Group 2 children each take the other end of a phone. Group 1 read out their messages slowly three times into the phone (preferably with everyone talking at the same time). After listening, group 2 have to decide whose message they think they've heard, take the paper from the child on the other end of their phone (without looking at it), and go and stand behind the child they've decided the message actually belonged to. Once they've made their choice they have to stick with it! How many have chosen correctly? Places can be switched, to see if group 1 can do as well.

THE SENSE OF TOUCH

HELP THE TRAVELLER HOME!

Set this up before the children enter the room, so that it forms the introduction to the whole parable.

> *You will need obstacles, such as chairs, boxes, a stepladder, a broom, pile of books, cushions, and so on, and three blindfolds.*

Lay the obstacles out in three rows (including one extra obstacle in each subsequent row). Choose three children to be the travellers, with one or two 'Samaritans' (depending on the number of children in the group) for each traveller.

Tell the travellers that they must rely on their Samaritan/s to get them over the obstacles.

While the three travellers are being carefully blindfolded, whisper to the Samaritans that each obstacle will be removed just before they reach it, but it's very important that they tell the traveller what the obstacle is, and pretend it's still there to be climbed over.

As the travellers start moving forwards, therefore, very quietly begin removing each obstacle just before it's reached. (Children not already occupied can help.) When the first traveller reaches 'home' they should be turned to face the way they've just come, and their blindfold immediately removed. They'll be amazed to see a clear floor in front of them. With extra obstacles in the other two rows, they, and the next traveller, will have the fun of seeing the non-existent obstacles being climbed over!

Helping someone often *does* mean removing the obstacles (problems and difficulties) before they get to them.

THANKS, BUT NO THANKS!

Helping each other sometimes means being their 'eyes' or 'hands'. But, to be a real help, we have to be sure we're doing what they actually need. (This is an amusing leaders' activity for the children to watch.)

> *You will need a large towel, items for washing, brushing hair, putting on face-cream, make-up and jewellery, or shaving, and a hand mirror.*

Make a play of a helper sitting another person down on a stool at a table with the above items laid out on it, and wrapping the towel around their shoulders, securing it at the back so it doesn't fall off. The person sitting down puts their own arms behind their backs, while the other person kneels behind them (so they clearly can't see what they're doing), rolling up their sleeves and replacing the other's arms and hands with their own. The more elaborate the hand-movements made by the 'helper', the better.

The person on the stool starts a dialogue, for example, 'Time to wash my face now... Ought to brush my hair…' and so on—but, of course, it won't be their hands making the actions. From time to time the one on the stool checks their mirror to see how 'well' it's going!

THE SENSE OF SMELL

WHOM CAN YOU TRUST?

The traveller had to *trust* the Samaritan that his offer of help was genuine. The Samaritan had to *trust* that the innkeeper would be honest about how much money he spent looking after the man, and the innkeeper had to *trust* that, if he spent more than the two silver coins, the Samaritan would return to pay the extra. That's an awful lot of trust, but it's a very, very important part of living. Not being able to trust the people around us must be awful. This is a 'trust' exercise, with a 'smelly' activity following on!

You will need one or three blindfolds (depending on the number of children available).

If there are enough children, divide them into three groups of five minimum (add leaders to make up numbers, if necessary), or use one group only. Choose one child to be blindfolded from each group, first letting all of them have a good smell of the three different odours which will be used in the 'Sniffing them out' activity below.

A circle is made around the blindfolded child, who stands feet together, arms folded over their chest, leaning gently against the shoulder-high raised palms of one of the others.

That child now gently pushes the blindfolded one towards one of the others in the group (all of whom also hold their hands at shoulder level, palms towards the centre child), who pushes back towards someone else in the circle, and so on.

It is extremely important that those in the circle support the centre child, who should feel safe at all times and able to trust the others not to let them fall.

Once the exercise is well established, the centre child can be swapped, so that others have a chance to experience that position.

At some point, you can start the activity below.

SNIFFING THEM OUT!

Wouldn't it be easier if the ones who can be the best kind of friend—who would really help and take care of us—had a special smell that we could recognize?

You will need a nice perfume (for the priest), an aftershave with a very different aroma (for the temple helper) and an antiseptic ointment, such as TCP (for the Samaritan).

While the trust exercise above is continuing, spray or dab the three separate smells on three of the children—either all in the one group, or one smell for one child in each group. Tell the blindfolded child that, when they think they're being touched by someone with one of the odours they smelt before the exercise began, they should call out 'STOP!', saying whether they think it's the priest, the temple helper, or the Samaritan.

Have they detected the right smell—and is it the right person? If only one group is being used, they need to try to find all three smells. This can be repeated one more time, before the smells start getting confused.

THE SENSE OF TASTE

WHO DESERVES A MEDAL?

The good Samaritan deserved a medal for going to so much trouble to help a complete stranger. The children can make themselves a medal, and it would be extra good if, beforehand, they could tell of something they've done recently to deserve it!

You will need:
- *Cooking chocolate (about 20g for each medal).*
- *Small round pastry cutters, baking trays and a large mixing bowl.*
- *Foil—preferably coloured, but ordinary tinfoil would be fine.*
- *Long, thin ribbons—enough for a metre length per medal.*
- *Sticky tape.*

Melt the chocolate in the bowl—preferably using a microwave, or you can place the bowl over a pan of hot water. Lay the pastry cutters out on the trays and pour about half a centimetre of melted chocolate into each one. Leave to cool and set. Gently push the chocolate discs out with thumbs and wrap each one in a piece of foil. Stick a metre-length of ribbon to the back of each medal, so that they can be hung around the children's necks.

If it's not possible for you to make the chocolate medals, use large, ready-made foil-covered coins instead.

HELPING EACH OTHER

The children have to work out how to help each other, otherwise no one will get any of the sweets!

You will need four teaspoons, attached with string or tape to the end of four long bamboo sticks, plus plenty of small sweets.

Ask for four volunteers. Stand them in a line, and give each a bamboo stick.

The volunteers should hold the sticks out in front of them, by the end opposite to the one with the spoon attached. Put a sweet in each spoon. Tell the children that the sweets are theirs to eat, but they've got to keep their hands where they are on the sticks. See how long it takes them to work out that, although they can't reach their own sweets, they can feed each other, and thus all get one. When they've discovered the answer, more sweets can be similarly handed around to the other children.

STEP INTO REFLECTION

As far as the injured man was concerned, because of the bad stories that were told about the people from Samaria, he would have expected to be attacked and robbed by a Samaritan, not helped by one. So how do the children think he'd have felt if he'd realized who it was bending over him on the desolate mountain road?

To help the children imagine this more vividly, ask one of them to pretend they've injured themselves badly. They should lie on the floor (they'll probably enjoy moaning and groaning in pain!).

One of the other children should then enter, dressed as scruffily as possible.

The scruffy child starts to offer to help the 'injured' one—but how does he or she feel about being approached by this person?

Have the children take turns to be the 'injured' and scruffy people.

There are times when we really need help in all sorts of different situations. We ask God to help, and we think that if he cares about us, he should answer our prayer. Well, he always does, but not necessarily in the way we choose or expect.

The children can help with this little sketch.

One of the leaders enters, carrying what appears to be an extremely heavy box. They put it on a table, or the floor, declaring that they can't carry it any further without some help, and then calling out loud for God to send someone to help them.

The smallest child in the group offers to help, but the leader says they're no good—they're far too small!

Then one of the other leaders, wearing a sling, offers to help, but is also turned away. *Two* good arms are needed, not just one!

Someone else—pretending to be rather old—offers help, but they're similarly rejected. Someone offers an imaginary wheelbarrow, but it's declared to be far too dirty (and squeaks too loudly as well).

'Give me ten minutes, and I'll be free to help' is another offer, but no, it's got to be this very minute!

The leader then picks up the 'enormously heavy' box again, grumbling and complaining that God never answers their prayers.

What do the children think? Did God answer the leader's prayer? Why didn't the leader think so?

STEP INTO PRAYER

Ask the children to write down something helpful that they might be asked to do, and the reasons (or excuses) they might give for not being able to do it. Then turn the suggestions into prayers, as below.

I SHOULDN'T MAKE EXCUSES!

Dear Jesus, It's more fun to (watch TV…), but help me to be generous and kind and do (the washing-up…) as well, or instead, when I'm asked to. I know that would make you happy —and my (mum / dad / brother / sister / gran / grandad / friend…) would be pretty pleased, too! Amen.

A couple of examples could be read out, but the children should take them home as a reminder of what they've said. Hopefully they'll offer help next time, rather than having to be asked.
   The prayer below can be printed out for the children to take home. It's called 'Excuses!'

*I asked Mum if she'd cook me a
boiled egg for breakfast.
She said she was already late for work,
so I went without.*

*I asked Dad if he'd play
football with me after school.
He said he had lots of phone calls to make,
so I played alone.*

*I asked my sister if she'd help me
with my homework.*

*She said she wanted to watch TV,
so I got the answers all wrong.*

*I asked my brother if he'd mend my bike.
He said he was going to meet his friends,
so the tyre stayed flat.*

*I went without, and I played alone, and I
made mistakes. I feel awfully flat!*

But…

*If I'd helped Mum a bit more,
she wouldn't have been late for work,
and she'd have had time to cook me a
boiled egg for breakfast.*

And…

*If I'd stopped watching TV earlier,
and asked Dad sooner,
he'd have been able to play
football with me.*

Or…

*If I'd helped my sister last week,
like she asked me to,
she'd probably have helped me this week.*

And then…

*If I learnt to mend my own bike,
I wouldn't have to bother my brother.*

*So I suppose I'd better stop
making excuses!*

STEP INTO THE STORY OF GOD'S KINGDOM

THE PARABLE OF THE TENANTS IN THE VINEYARD

MATTHEW 21:33–46

OLD TESTAMENT LINK

Recognizing who is the true king.

This parable could be introduced by doing the 'I promise!' activity on page 139.

The chief priests and leaders were not happy! In fact, they were getting pretty angry. Jesus had been telling people about God for nearly three years and wherever he went people flocked around him, anxious to hear his every word. He was becoming a definite threat to the chief priests' and leaders' authority and control, and something serious would have to be done about that.

Jesus knew exactly what they were thinking. Was he afraid? Of course not! He was going to tell everyone the truth about God, whether the authorities liked it or not. And so, when the priests and leaders were nearby one day, he told them to listen to this story.

'A land owner,' he said, 'once planted a vineyard. He built a wall around it and dug a pit to crush the grapes in. He also built a lookout tower, so that it could be protected. It was clearly worth a lot of money! Now the owner had other business in another country, so he paid tenants to run the vineyard for him. They could take some of the profit for themselves, of course, but agreed to give the owner his fair share of each grape harvest.

'So, when the first harvest time came around, the owner arranged for his servants to go to the vineyard and collect his share of the grapes. But the tenants, unfortunately, turned out to be very wicked people. They'd decided that they wanted to keep all of the grapes for themselves, so they beat up one of the servants, stoned another and even killed a third servant. When the owner heard what had happened, he decided to send a larger number of servants to collect his grapes. They'd surely sort out the problem! But the tenants treated this second group as badly as the first. So still the owner got none of his harvest.

'The owner must have been furious by that time. He decided the only thing to do was to send his own son. Surely the tenants would respect him? But he was wrong. As soon as the tenants saw the son approaching, they said to themselves, "One day this man will own the vineyard. We can keep the whole place for ourselves if we kill him now." And so that's what they did.'

Then Jesus turned to the chief priests and leaders and asked, 'When the owner of that vineyard arrives, what do you suppose he will do to those tenants?' The chief priests and leaders answered, 'He'll kill them in some horrible way, of course. Then he'll let his vineyard to people who will give him his share of grapes at harvest time.'

'Quite right,' Jesus said, 'and God's kingdom is just like that vineyard, with God as the owner. God's kingdom will be taken away from you and given to people who will do what he asks!'

Well, the authorities certainly didn't like that. They were powerfully in control of all the ceremonies and sacrifices that took place in the temple and were determined to keep things that way. This Jesus, they thought, was just a trouble-maker. They would have to find an excuse to arrest him and get rid of him for good. But by now a huge number of the people believed that Jesus was the most special person they'd ever met (which, of course, he was).

It was a big problem.

STEP INTO THE SENSES

THE SENSE OF SIGHT

THE WHOLE PICTURE

The chief priests and leaders couldn't see the truth of God's love any more. And they couldn't see that Jesus was their friend and Saviour. When they looked at him they just saw an enemy and a danger to their way of life. It's far easier for us now to see what a wonderful person Jesus is, but it's much harder to recognize things when you only see a little bit of the picture.

> *You will need:*
> - *A5 sheets of paper rolled up tightly and stuck, to make very narrow tubes (one per child).*
> - *Lots of lightweight items, such as small cuddly toys, a book, a ball, an artificial flower, plastic mug, cushion, roll of sticky tape, pencil, and so on.*
> - *Drapes for two chairs.*

The two chairs should be set about a metre and a half apart, and draped so that the children can't see behind them. A leader should be crouched behind each chair. One of the leaders has a box with all the items inside.

Sit the children on the floor a little distance away from the chairs. As they look through their paper tube 'telescope' (with the other eye tightly closed), the leader with the items in a box throws them one by one to the leader behind the other chair, who (hopefully!) catches them. The children should call out what they think the item was.

How many did they see correctly? Repeat without the tube 'telescopes'. How much easier is it to see things clearly when they have the whole picture?

CATCH US IF YOU CAN!

The second lot of servants, knowing what had happened to the first, must have felt a bit worried about how they'd be treated. What would the children have done? Perhaps they'd have tried to get inside the vineyard and take the owner's grapes without getting caught by the wicked tenants.

> *You will need chalk, or similar, to draw a line on the floor as the boundary of the 'vineyard', plus a bowl of seedless grapes (or sweets) on a table inside the 'vineyard'.*

One of the leaders becomes the 'tenant', standing on the boundary of the vineyard with his/her back to the children. In groups of no more than six, the 'servants' have to try to get across the boundary and into the vineyard without getting caught by the tenant. As they creep towards the line, they must stop dead in their tracks the moment the tenant turns towards them, which s/he does at will. Which of the servants will be the first to get a grape (or sweet)?

THE SENSE OF SOUND

QUIET AS A MOUSE!

The tenants in the vineyard wanted to keep everything for themselves. That was very wrong, and the owner's servants would have done their best to take away what belonged to their master, without getting hurt.

> *You will need a collection of items laid out on a couple of tables (those used in 'The whole picture' activity on page 137 would be fine, but the children can add some of their own personal things, if they wish), plus a couple of rolled-up newspapers and two blindfolds.*

Two children are chosen to be the tenants and should sit behind the table with their blindfolds on, each holding a rolled-up newspaper. The other children are the servants. They stand at the far side of the room (their base) and must creep up and try to take one of the items. If the tenant hears someone, they should try to (gently) swat them before they can retrieve anything. If caught, the servant returns to base empty-handed and starts again. The winning servants are the two with the most items. They can then become the next tenants and repeat the activity.

CAN YOU HEAR ME?

The chief priests and leaders had been given plenty of time to listen to what Jesus was saying and recognize him as their true king. But although they certainly did *listen*, they didn't allow themselves to *hear* the wonderful messages. It was as though they were too far away to be able to hear the words properly.

One of the leaders decides upon a message they'd like to give the children. For example:

• There's a whistle on the windowsill. Go and blow it.
• Shout 'Hooray!' nice and loudly.
• Jump up and down on the spot.
• Run twice around the room.

The children sit on chairs in a row, listening hard, while the leader moves very slowly towards them saying the message very softly. Who is really listening, manages to hear the words first, and then acts on them? Repeat, using one of the other messages.

THE SENSE OF TOUCH

SOMETHING SPECIAL

The religious leaders allowed themselves to be treated as if they were extra-special human beings. With this parable, Jesus was reminding them that it was God who should be worshipped, not them.

Unfortunately, we're no better today. Now we choose sport, film, pop and TV soap stars to worship, as if they were somehow different from the rest of us—which they aren't! The only really super-special person who's ever lived is Jesus.

> *You will need items as collected for the 'Heaven and earth' activity on page 112, including the roll of wallpaper, glue and sticky tape.*

From the wallpaper, cut two very large standing figures. One represents Jesus, and the other represents everyone else. The children should cover the figure of Jesus with the smooth, soft, shiny and bright items, creating a figure that not only looks colourful but is very nice to touch. The other figure—'humankind'—should be covered with the dull and rough items that do not feel so good. The figures can be put up on the wall, with a notice beside them encouraging anyone passing by to use their sense of touch to experience the difference between us and Jesus!

FEEL THE DIFFERENCE!

Every single one of us is special to God, and it's amazing to think that he knew each one of us even before we were born. Jesus said that God even notices every bird that falls to the ground. But how much notice do we take of each other?

Ask the children to close their eyes. Then mention an item of clothing that one of the leaders is wearing. Can the children say what colour it is? They probably won't know! So how well do they know each other? They recognize each other when they can see, but how about when they can't?

> *You will need a blindfold.*

One child is chosen to be blindfolded, and, at the start of the activity, must catch one of the other children who are running slowly around. The blindfolded child then feels the other's face and tries to say who it is that they've caught. Whether or not they're right, the blindfold is passed to the child who was caught. Afterwards the children can say how difficult or easy they found this to do. If they were correctly identified, how did that make them feel?

THE SENSE OF SMELL

I PROMISE!

The tenants must have made all sorts of promises about the share of the harvest they would give to the owner when the time came. He believed that they would keep those promises but sadly they didn't. Instead, they gave him nothing at all.

> *You will need:*
> - *Some nice-smelling sweets, such as fudge, chocolate, coconut, mint, fruit sweets, and so on, each wrapped in a thin twist of coloured tissue paper.*
> - *Rolled-up bits of paper, similarly wrapped so that they look like the sweets.*
> - *A box to dip in to, with a bright notice on it, listing the above sweets.*

One of the leaders invites a child up and says, 'I promise that I will give you…' and mentioning one of the sweets. The child then dips their hand in the box, smells what they bring out and tries to decide if they've got what the leader promised. Or can they smell something different? They unwrap what they've got. If they guessed right, they get to keep the sweet. If they guessed wrong, the sweet is given to someone else. But, of course, if there was no sweet at all, no one gets anything.

Continue as required, making sure everyone finally does get a sweet!

RECOGNIZING THE TRUTH

The owner of the vineyard could have gone to collect his grapes himself, rather than sending servants and then his own son. But, in spite of everything, he trusted the tenants to do the right thing. However, in the end he had to find out the truth for himself.

> *You will need raw pieces of apple, pear, potato and parsnip, all looking as similar as possible, one large plate for each of the above (one type on each plate), cocktail sticks, and a card with the above four items listed on it.*

Stick cocktail sticks into all the pieces of food, and put the plates on a table. Prop the card up, to remind the children which four smells they're trying to identify.

A leader sits next to the table, pretending to be asleep. One at a time, the children creep up to the tray and quickly take a piece of food. (Mostly they should be allowed to do this, though every so often the leader can pretend to wake up and make a fuss about them 'stealing' the food.)

When they've got a piece they run back, smell it, say (with great confidence!) what they think they've taken and pass it to a couple of the others

to smell. The others smell the piece of food and decide whether they think they've been told the truth, or whether they think it's one of the others. A leader should make the final decision.

Repeat as often as required.

THE SENSE OF TASTE

MAKING THE RIGHT CHOICE

When the owner of the vineyard chose his tenants, he obviously thought he'd made a good choice and trusted them to be honest. Unfortunately, he was very wrong. But sometimes, sadly, it's very easy to be fooled by other people.

> *You will need, in separate boxes which all look the same, some icing sugar, cornflour, sherbet, salt, custard powder and white flour.*

Mark on the base of the box which item is which. Make one card for each of the above items.

Lay the boxes out on a table, propping the cards up beside each one but making sure that half of them have the wrong cards. Invite one of the children up and ask them to take, say, the 'icing sugar' box. That child then goes to someone else in the group, inviting them to dip their finger in and taste the 'icing sugar'. If they agree with the taste, they put the box back beside the icing sugar card. If they think they've tasted something different, they return the box to its place but switch cards. Do this six times so that every card finishes up beside the correct box. Or will they?

This can be repeated, mixing the cards up again each time.

FULL OF SURPRISES!

You couldn't take anything for granted with Jesus because he was rarely what people expected him to be. Instead he was full of surprises, and a very exciting person indeed.

You will need:
- *Slices of bread, cut into quarters.*
- *Ordinary knives for spreading and cutting.*
- *A variety of fillings that the children can 'mix and match', for example, cheese, honey, jam, peanut butter, marmalade, ketchup, chocolate strands, cucumber, tomato, wafer-thin ham, and so on.*

The children put together one mini-sandwich each, choosing some exciting new fillings. The leaders then ask each child a question from the parable. For example:

- Why didn't the owner look after the vineyard himself?
- How many servants did the owner first send?
- What happened to them?
- Then what did the owner do?
- Why did the tenants decide to kill the son?
- What did the priests say the owner would do when he got to the vineyard?
- Why didn't the priests like this parable?

- What did they decide to do about Jesus?
- What did the ordinary people think about Jesus?

If the child gets the answer wrong, they have to eat their own sandwich. If they get it right, the leader has to eat it—and try to say what the surprise filling is!

STEP INTO REFLECTION

This simple dialogue needs two narrators who direct the questions towards the children.

Narrator 1: You know, the exciting thing about parables is that they tell one simple story…

Narrator 2: …about sheep, or farmers, or vineyard owners…

Narrator 1: …but there's always another 'real life' message wrapped up inside.

Narrator 2: Just like clues in a mystery story.

Narrator 1: For instance, the owner of the vineyard sent his son to collect the harvest. He thought the tenants would respect him, and treat him properly.

Narrator 2: Instead, they killed him.

Narrator 1: Jesus said that God is like the vineyard owner and we're the harvest.

Narrator 2: So what was the clue Jesus was giving them about himself?

Narrator 1: But did the owner give up on his vineyard and just forget all about it?

Narrator 2: No. So what does that tell us about God?

Narrator 1: Jesus was giving the leaders and chief priests a bit of a hard time. Does that mean they were bad people?

Narrator 2: Not really, but there were a huge number of them. It wasn't like today, with only (name the clergy in your church). How many priests do you think would arrive in Jerusalem for a feast such as Passover in Jesus' day?

Narrator 1: A lot more than that! There was the high priest, some 200 chief priests, about 7,200 ordinary priests and nearly 10,000 temple workers (the Levites)!

Narrator 2: Wow! Sounds like worshipping God had turned into big business.

Narrator 1: That's right. Everyone had a very special job to do, and it had to be done exactly right.

Narrator 2: So I guess the chief priests and leaders thought they were pretty important people. They made the rules. The people, sort of, belonged to them.

Narrator 1: And that's another clue! That was why Jesus told this parable about tenants of a vineyard who thought that, as they were doing all the work in growing the grapes, they ought to be allowed to keep everything for themselves.

Narr. 1 and 2: Were they right, do you think?

STEP INTO PRAYER

This is a prayer that could be presented at an all-age service.

Actions can be included. The children can rock an imaginary boat, shake their closed hands, jump up and down and join in with shouting, 'You shouldn't do that!'

Also, if the children have one letter each for the phrase, 'GOD IS LOVE', printed on card and pinned to their backs, they can move—or be moved—around until, with their backs to the congregation, they form a line revealing those words at the two relevant points in the prayer.

JESUS TOLD THE TRUTH, NO MATTER WHAT THE COST

Jesus told the truth, no matter what the cost to himself.
He wasn't afraid of 'rocking the boat',
or shaking ideas around in the palms of his hands
until all the bad ones fell out.
He was good at jumbling up thoughts
then putting them back together again
so they said
GOD IS LOVE.
He wasn't afraid to go jumping up and down in the temple
and shouting, 'You shouldn't do that!'
Jesus didn't try to agree with everybody.
He wanted us to think for ourselves.
He didn't follow the rich and the famous
and say how great they were.
He went and had tea with those who were rough, poor, or sick,
the ones nobody else liked,
and the ones who got things wrong a lot of the time,
but were very sorry.
Yes, he was good at jumbling up thoughts
then putting them back together again
so they said
GOD IS LOVE.

Perhaps the children can add a verse of their own.

Chapter 18

STEP INTO THE STORY OF GOD'S LOVE

THE PARABLE OF THE PRODIGAL SON

LUKE 15:11–32

OLD TESTAMENT LINK

God never gives up on us.

This is a great parable! It shows how God never gives up on us. There was a man, Jesus said, who had two sons. Together they ran the family farm, but one day the younger son decided he wanted the chance to do something more exciting with his life, so he said to his father, 'Give me my share of what the farm is worth.'

Well, his father loved his son, so he did as he was asked. Not long after that, the young son packed up everything he owned and left for a foreign country. Now he'd have a good time! Sadly, though, he didn't care how much he spent or wasted, and pretty soon nothing was left—not a single penny.

As if that wasn't bad enough, then there spread through that whole country a very bad famine. So now, even if he'd had the money, there was very little food to buy. Still, he had to survive and eventually found a job looking after pigs. But, do you know, the pigs ate better than he did! He often looked at the food they got and wished he could have as much. But no one gave him a thing.

One day the son was mucking out those pigs, and feeling pretty miserable and extremely hungry, when he had a sudden thought: 'My father's workers have plenty to eat, and here I am, starving to death! I'll go to him, admit how wrong I've been, and ask for his pity. I'm not good enough to be called his son any more, but becoming one of his workers will be better than living like this!'

So he immediately set out on the long journey back home. It took weeks, but finally he climbed wearily over the very last hill and there at last was his father's farm.

Now, what he didn't know was that every day he'd been gone, his father had longed for his return. When suddenly a figure appeared on the horizon he just knew it was his son—in spite of how thin he was! Stopping what he was doing, he ran to meet him, hugging and kissing him for joy. But the son hung his head and said, 'No, father, you mustn't treat me like this. I'm no longer good enough to be called your son!' Did his father take any notice? Of course not! He called out to his servants, 'Find the best clothes for my son, and prepare a grand feast. We must celebrate his safe return!'

But not everyone was happy. Remember the older son? He'd stayed at home and always worked really hard, but there were never any celebrations for him. He felt so hurt and angry, he refused even to go into the house. His father came out and begged him to join in the celebrations, but he said, 'I've worked like one of your slaves for years, and have never done anything wrong, yet you've never so much as given me a little goat so I could give a dinner for my friends. But my brother comes home after wasting all your money and you order the best calf to be killed for a feast!'

His father smiled and said, 'Everything I have is yours, you know that. But I thought your brother was dead and lost for ever. Now he's come home. How can we do anything less than celebrate?'

And God, of course, is just like that father. What a wonderful thought!

STEP INTO THE SENSES

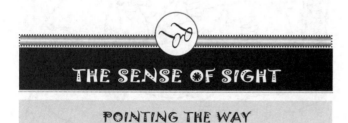

THE SENSE OF SIGHT

POINTING THE WAY

The prodigal son wanted to find his way home. God is our real home, but finding our way to him can be difficult. We have to watch that we don't go in the wrong direction.

> *You will need a large octagon-shaped piece of paper, plus smaller ones for each of the children.*

Create the octagon shape by folding a square piece of paper in half, then in half again so that you still have a square. Bring the two folded edges together to make a triangle. Position the triangle in front of you, as shown in figure 4. Measure the top edge and mark the same distance along the diagonal edge. Cut between those points and throw the spare paper away. Unfold to reveal the octagon. You now have a compass with a difference! Write the word GOD, and an arrow pointing outwards, along the north-west fold (see Figure 5).

Moving the top towards you, so that it becomes the bottom, turn the octagon over, and again write GOD and an arrow along the north-west fold. Turn the paper over a few times to show the children that the way to God is always pointing in the same direction on back and front.

Move the octagon round so that the arrow points north-east. Turn the paper over (top towards you) and the arrow on the back will be pointing in the opposite direction! Again, move the octagon to show the arrow in a different position, turn it over, and each time the arrow on the back will be pointing in an unexpected direction. The children can now have a go.

The back and front arrows remain in the same position when the octagon is turned, only when they point either north-west or south-east, so it could be said that this little activity reminds us that God is always on the same straight pathway: even if we try to turn away from him, he will always be there waiting for us to get back on the right path.

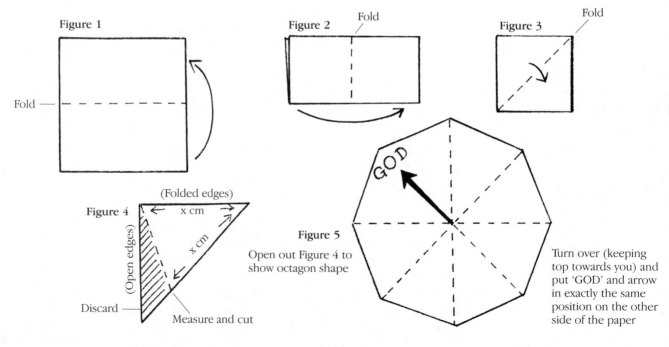

Figure 1

Fold

Figure 2

Fold

Figure 3

Fold

Figure 4

(Folded edges)

x cm

x cm

(Open edges)

Discard

Measure and cut

Figure 5

Open out Figure 4 to show octagon shape

GOD

Turn over (keeping top towards you) and put 'GOD' and arrow in exactly the same position on the other side of the paper

HOW MUCH DO I LOVE YOU?

The dad in this parable loved both his children very much. God loves *us* so much that he was willing for Jesus to die on the cross for all the things we do wrong. To remind ourselves how much Jesus loves us, we can spread wide our arms, as Jesus had to on the cross, and say, 'This much!' But when we do that we're also holding *ourselves* between our fingertips. That's something worth thinking about!

You will need two or three tape measures.

Get the shortest and tallest two children to spread their arms wide, as Jesus did on the cross. Measure the distance from fingertip to fingertip. Note the measurements. Then measure the two children's heights. You will discover that their height exactly matches the distance between their fingertips. The other children will probably want to check their heights in this way.

Try this too: if the children measure the distance from their wrist-bone to their elbow they'll discover that it exactly matches the size of their feet!

alter the sounds that can be created when the bottles or pots are shaken, rolled, or tapped against each other. Using your shakers and drums, experiment with different ways to build up the sound and then create a disco-style party beat to dance to.

THE SENSE OF SOUND

SHAKE, RATTLE AND ROLL!

The father wanted to celebrate his son's return—just as there are celebrations in heaven, Jesus says, when we find our way to God. Noisy ones would be the nicest, and funny noises are the best of all. Let's experiment with different party sounds!

You will need:
- *Small plastic drinks bottles, or yoghurt pots with lids, plus dry rice, beans, macaroni, small stones or beads.*
- *Sticky tape for sealing up the yoghurt pot lids.*
- *Small empty boxes, ranging from cheese boxes to grocery boxes, to make drums.*

Put some of the dry ingredients into the bottles or pots. Different amounts and different contents

EMPTY-HANDED?

While his money lasted, the prodigal son had been used to having everything he wanted, just when he wanted it. But once he'd wasted all the money, he was fortunate if he got anything at all—and very often he went empty-handed.

You will need plenty of balloons in different colours, some yellow, some blue, some green and some red, plus a basket, or baskets, to collect the balloons in.

One child is chosen to be the prodigal son, and stands in the middle of the circle. (If there are a lot of children, split the group into smaller circles with one 'son' per circle.) The others are given a few inflated balloons, some of each colour.

At a signal, the children pat the balloons across the circle to each other. The prodigal son has to try to catch the balloons. When he or she catches a balloon, it is placed in a basket outside the circle. After all the balloons have been caught, or after a set time, the prodigal son can see what, if anything, he has managed to get for himself. Places can be switched, so that all the children have a go at being the piggy in the middle.

Use the colours of the balloons to represent items that the son needs as follows:

• Yellow: food
• Blue: water
• Red: clothing
• Green: a mattress to sleep on

THE SENSE OF TOUCH

GET HIM DRESSED!

The father was so delighted to see his son safely back home that he sent his servants off to bring the very best clothes for him to wear.

> *You will need two pillow cases, each containing one set of clothes including a large T-shirt, a pair of trousers, coat, hat, scarf, gloves, boots or large wellies, plus a large card with these items listed in order.*

Divide the children into two teams, with their pair of pillow cases at the end of the room. Prop or pin up the list of items near the pillow cases. Each team chooses their 'prodigal son' and 'father'. The rest are 'servants'.

The first 'servant' in each team has to retrieve the first item in the above list from one of their pillow cases—by *feel* only—then run back and give it to the 'father', who puts the item of clothing on the 'son'. When the son has been dressed in that item of clothing, the next servant runs to get the next item on the list.

When the prodigal son is fully 'dressed', he or she runs back to the empty pillow case and holds it above his or her head. The first team to complete the game is the winner, but whether they think they're wearing the 'best' clothes is another matter!

FINDING THE WAY HOME

There were no maps to follow or road signs to show you the way in New Testament times—and no street lights, either, when it began to get dark. All the prodigal son's senses would have been needed to help him find his way on the long journey back home.

> *You will need:*
> • *Various items that might be encountered on a journey across the land, such as a small branch with leaves, a piece of tree bark, a rock, sheep's wool, abandoned bird's nest, flowers, a mushroom, corn or wheat, grass, moss, weeds, ivy, a (clean and empty!) snail shell, an apple, chestnuts, fir cone, and so on.*
> • *A skipping rope, a small blanket and noisy items, such as a bell, tambourine, or whistle.*
> • *One blindfold.*

One child at a time can volunteer to be the prodigal son and wears the blindfold. The other children form a zigzag 'pathway' around the room.

Give the rope to two children, who stand at the head of the 'pathway'. Give the blanket to two more and things from the suggested list to all the others. Give the last two children in the zigzag the noisy items. The 'son' must find his or her way 'home' by feeling the way over the rope, crawling under the blanket (children holding these items shouldn't make this difficult), guessing the items held out by others, and following the sounds of the noisy items. When he or she reaches the end of the 'pathway' the game can be repeated with a different 'son' (also changing the items from the suggested list).

THE SENSE OF SMELL

SMELLS FAMILIAR?

The prodigal son made the difficult journey to a different country because he wanted to experience new and exciting things. Today, we don't even have to go out of our own country to experience what food from far-distant places smells and tastes like.

You will need:
- *'Exotic' fruit and vegetables, cut into small pieces or mashed up, and put on separate plates. For example, use mango, passion fruit, avocado, aubergine, root or crystallized ginger, kiwi fruit, sweet potato, mange-tout, yellow or orange pepper, coconut, lime, dates, figs.*
- *Cards with each of the items used written on them.*

As a group, or as individuals, the children can try to place the cards correctly in front of each of the plates, using their sense of smell. How many of these items are familiar to them? This activity can be followed up by going straight into the 'Tastes familiar?' activity on page 150.

THE SMELL OF A STORM!

The prodigal son must have had to cope with all sorts of different weather and conditions on his long journey back home.

You will need tissues on, or in, similar containers, smelling of the following:
- *Antiseptic (Action: fall down a hill).*
- *Deodorant (Action: climb up a hill).*
- *Vanilla essence (Action: feeling very hot).*
- *Chocolate (Action: feeling very cold).*
- *Fish paste (Action: swim across a river).*
- *Grass cuttings (Action: wade through long grass).*
- *Mix of all the above (Action: run—it's a big storm!).*

Everyone stands in the middle of the room. The containers are placed on a table at the far end. Work through the above list with everyone, practising the actions.

Choose the first child to run to the table, smell one of the containers/tissues, and call out what they think the smell is. (It doesn't matter if they get the smell wrong—though they should try to get it right!) They then run back to join the others.

As soon as the smell has been called out, everyone must try to remember what that smell means and act accordingly. The more elaborate the actions, the better! Whoever is last to get the action right should be the next to guess a smell. If necessary, move the containers around between turns.

THE SENSE OF TASTE

TASTES FAMILIAR?

The further away from home the prodigal son went, the more unfamiliar everything would have seemed to him—especially the food. But he couldn't do what some people do today—go to the other side of the world and still only eat roast beef or fish and chips. He'd have had to get used to the taste of lots of unusual things.

> *You will need the 'exotic' fruit and vegetables as prepared for the 'Smells familiar?' activity on page 149, this time on separate plates and covered with paper napkins.*

Invite the children to experience the unusual flavours and textures of the food, by selecting an item from beneath the napkins and, without looking at it, trying to identify it from the taste alone.

If they did the 'Smells familiar' activity, ask which was easier, identifying the item by smell or by taste? Did they have a favourite flavour? Were they put off the flavour by the texture of some of the foods? Which foods that are familiar to us might seem strange and unpleasant to people from different countries?

BEFORE AND AFTER!

By the time he finally got back home, the prodigal son must have looked rather as if he'd been stranded for ages on a desert island, with no food or fresh clothing!

> *You will need:*
> * *Some ready-made gingerbread figures.*
> * *Smooth jam, and knives for spreading.*
> * *A variety of small sweets, sugar and chocolate strands or sprinkles, licorice 'laces', raisins, candied fruit, desiccated coconut and so on.*

The children can choose to decorate their gingerbread figure as a modern-day prodigal son (or daughter), looking either as he or she might look when first arriving back home, or very smart and tidy after they've been dressed in the very best of clothes.

The jam will create a 'sticky' surface, and the children can then use the suggested items to create smart or torn clothing, a fancy hat (or long, scruffy hair), shoes, boots (or bare feet), a happy or miserable face and rings (or bandages!) for the fingers.

STEP INTO REFLECTION

We might try to separate ourselves from God, but he never separates himself from us. The children can remind themselves of that in this simple way.

> *You will need a 4cm x 30 cm strip of paper.*

Write 'GOD' and 'ME' close to the edge of opposite long sides of the strip, so that you can see both the words but they're spread apart. Hold the strip at each end. Make a half twist of one end of the paper, then stick the two ends together. Now cut round the centre of the ring. The result isn't two rings, as you'd expect, but 'GOD' and 'ME' are now part of one big ring!

Now cut round the centre again (making sure you don't chop off the top of either word!). Has this now made an even bigger ring? No, now you'll see you have two rings, and 'GOD' and 'ME' are still on the same one!

MAKING THE HEADLINES

Let's step back in time, and see what the *Jerusalem Times* was saying in 33BC.

MISSING SON RETURNS

In an exultant reunion today, Philip, younger son of Moab, and missing for two years, suddenly reappeared as if from nowhere. Philip, dubbed 'the prodigal son' by neighbours (nothing to do with being a child prodigy—sources confirm that 'prodigal' means someone who wastes money), has certainly lived up to the name since, by all accounts, he has returned utterly penniless. Readers will recall that he left with a half-share of the entire family estate, which must have been worth a serious shekel or two. He also returned very, very thin—and smelling rather strongly of pig, which no doubt accounts for the fact that his father, having initially hugged him warmly, hurriedly decided he needed a complete change of clothes and several hot showers.

Friends of the elder brother, Mark, say that he was not best pleased when his father insisted on killing the fatted calf in celebration of his brother's return. 'He's never even given me so much as a beefburger,' he was heard to complain rather sulkily. 'And I've been such a good boy, too!'

However, as Moab delightedly explained, 'I thought my son was dead and lost for ever. How can I *not* celebrate? Besides, he's already punished himself enough. I certainly don't need to!'

With that statement, as the unmistakable odour of swine follows Philip relentlessly around the village, this reporter simply has to agree.

The children might like to think about what, in this story, would have been important to them, as news reporters of the day. What would they have written for the 33BC *Jerusalem Times*?

STEP INTO PRAYER

God is always looking out for us to come home to him. He'll come and meet us halfway, too. It's never too late to turn to him—and he'll always be really glad to see us!

IT'S TIME I GOT AWAY FROM HERE

It's time I got away from here.
It's time I got a life!
I get so bored—standing about waiting for
something to happen.

I know I'm supposed to be
patient and good
and obey all the rules.
But there are far too many of those!

Like: Don't do that! Don't go there!
Don't make a noise! Don't make a mess!
Sit still! Don't stare! Do this job!
Clean that up! Finish this!

Why so many orders?
Why so many rules?

Maybe if I go there, it'll be different.
Maybe over there will be
more fun than here,
and I'll be able to do what I choose.
Or do nothing at all!
I think I'll try it.
Right now!

But I know, I really do know,
that if I get in a muddle,
and there is not as good as here,

and all the people I thought were my
friends suddenly disappear from view
and I have nothing left at all,
I can call out to Jesus and he'll
come and find me—
even when nobody else can.
He'll come out to meet me,
give me a huge hug,
and walk with me to where there's love.
And then there'll be a big, big party.

But something tells me that I don't have to
leave home to find all that.
It's right here.
Beside me.
RIGHT NOW!

Chapter 19

STEP INTO THE STORY OF GOD'S JUSTICE

THE PARABLE OF THE UNFORGIVING SERVANT

MATTHEW 18:21–35

OLD TESTAMENT LINK

God punishes us justly for our deeds.

How good are you at forgiving friends who do something to you that you don't like? Maybe it's borrowing your best pen, then 'forgetting' to give it back. Or keeping secrets from you. Or making fun of you because you're no good at sports. You might forgive them three or four times, but after that you probably won't be friends with them any more.

Peter, one of the disciples, asked Jesus one day, 'How many times should I forgive someone who does something wrong against me? Is seven times enough?' He probably thought that was pretty generous but Jesus said that seventy-seven times was more like it. In other words, Peter (and each of us) should never stop forgiving other people. I imagine Peter looked pretty dismayed at that answer. So Jesus decided to tell this story.

There was once a king who allowed some of his top officials to borrow money from him whenever they needed to (there were no banks for people to borrow money from in those days, of course). To make sure the loans were being regularly repaid, the king would, from time to time, ask each official to report to him how much they still owed. Everything was going fine until he discovered that one of the officials owed him many thousands of silver coins. One silver coin would have been a whole day's wage for an ordinary worker, so that was a *huge* amount! Well, the king was furious that the man had borrowed so much, and even angrier when the official said that he didn't have any money to pay back the loan. So the king ordered him to be sold—along with his wife and children and everything he owned—in order to pay the debt. That wasn't an unusual thing to do in those days, but it sounds pretty awful, doesn't it? It did to the official, too, and so he got down on his knees and started begging. 'Have pity on me,' he pleaded, 'and I will pay you every penny I owe!'

Now the king, being actually very kind and generous, felt sorry for the man, so he not only let him go free but also told him he didn't have to pay back a single penny. Can you imagine that? The official must have been very happy indeed. So happy that, on leaving the king and meeting another official—someone who owed him a mere hundred silver coins—he immediately told this other man to forget his debt altogether... Well, that's what *should* have happened. Except that he wasn't kind and generous like the king. Instead, he grabbed the man by the throat and shouted, 'Pay me what you owe!'

Well, the man got down on his knees and begged, 'Have pity on me, and I will pay you back.' But the first official refused to have pity. Instead, he went and had the man put in jail until he could pay what he owed.

Now, when some of the other people in the king's court heard about this, they felt very sorry for the man who'd been put in jail, and decided to tell the king what had happened. As you can imagine, the king wasn't at all pleased. He called for the official and said, 'You are an evil man! When you begged for mercy, I said you didn't have to pay back a penny. Don't you think you should show pity to someone else, as I did to you?' The king was so angry, in fact, that he ordered the official to be tortured until he could pay back everything he owed.

So, Jesus told Peter, you must learn to forgive each other with all of your heart.

STEP INTO THE SENSES

THE SENSE OF SIGHT

DISAPPEARING DEBT

The king was extremely generous in allowing the official's debt just to 'disappear'. The children can do the same thing in this activity.

You will need:
- *Ready-cut cardboard circles, divided into seven equal sections on each side and with two small holes cut on either side of the centre (the children could make the holes).*
- *Paints in the colours red, orange, yellow, green, blue, indigo and violet. (Extra colours can easily be created from the primary colours red, yellow and blue: blue and yellow = green; red and yellow = orange; blue and red = violet; blue and violet = indigo.)*
- *Lengths of wool or thin string.*

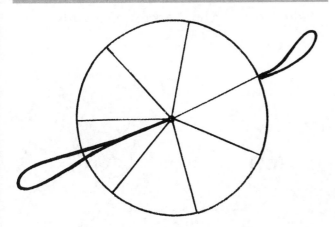

Using the colours in the order given above, print the following letters in each of the seven sections: FI - FT - Y - TH - OU - SA - ND. Do the same on the other side, matching the colours in each section.

Thread the wool through both holes in the card. Tie the ends together to make a long loop. Holding an end of the loop in each hand fairly tautly, the children should twirl their hands in a circle until the wool is well twisted. Then, moving their hands together and apart, the disc will start to spin. Now they can see that they've made the 'FIFTY THOUSAND' disappear!

Can any of the children say why this has happened? (White light is made up of these colours. When they're spun together quickly, our eyes can only see the total colour—white. In effect, they've made the opposite of a rainbow!)

GET WRIGGLING!

The official who owed all that money wasn't a nice man at all, and he very nearly managed to wriggle out of paying even so much as a penny of his debt.

You will need one strip of kitchen paper (about 10 cm x 30 cm) per child, one long pencil or small garden cane per child, and water.

Roll the rectangle of kitchen paper around the pencil so that it forms a tube. Push down one edge of the paper, at the same time squeezing it carefully along the pencil from the other end till it's pushed into a tubular 'concertina' in the middle of the pencil. Slip the tube off the pencil and drip one or two drops of water on it. The paper will become like a wriggling snake, stretching and writhing about in an amazing way.

THE SENSE OF SOUND

You will need to create one area (beyond the king) to represent becoming free from the debt, and a line of chairs at the other end of the room to represent the prison or jail.

One of the leaders is the king, and stands with their back to the children. The children stand facing the king but with their backs to the chairs, and start creeping towards the king who, without any warning, will suddenly turn and say, 'Pay me now!' or 'Pay me nothing!' or 'Pay me or go to jail!'

If the children hear the first command, they must stop in their tracks; the second, they can continue moving forwards; and the last, they must start walking backwards towards the chairs (the prison). Anyone who makes the wrong move has to take a step backwards. Whoever manages to get past the king is free. Whoever reaches the chairs must go to 'prison'.

UNDER HIS NOSE

It's one thing to take pity on someone and decide to cancel their debt, but it's quite another thing to be tricked out of what is rightfully yours. The king very nearly had thousands of silver coins stolen from under his very nose!

You will need a large box of cornflakes or similar cereal, a metal tray, lots of small denomination coins, and a blindfold.

Someone is chosen to be the 'king', and sits blindfolded on a chair in front of the others, with the tray of coins (which have been made into as tall a pile as possible) at his or her feet. Sprinkle plenty of cornflakes over the floor between the king and the others, so that the children have to walk over that area to reach the tray at the king's feet. (Lay newspaper down first if your floor area is carpeted.)

Divide the children into groups of three. Position the three groups so that they have the same distance to go, but approach the king from different angles, trying not to make any noise. If the king hears something, he or she shouts, 'Stop!' and the children stop in their tracks. The king points in the direction of the noise. If he or she is pointing directly at a child, that person is out. If any children make it as far as the tray, they should try to take as many coins as they can before the king realizes they're there. The next group can then have a go. Who retrieves the most coins?

An important part of the activity is for the children to sweep up the cereal afterwards!

THE SENSE OF TOUCH

HOW MUCH DO YOU OWE?

There was a rule in Jesus' day that, if a debt had remained unpaid for seven years, it was cancelled altogether. That was why the king needed to make regular checks to find out how much each official owed, and whether they had enough to pay the money back.

> *You will need cards showing different amounts of money (two cards for every amount).*

One child is chosen to be the king. All the others are given a card, which they must hold against themselves so the king cannot see it. (NB: There needs to be an even number of children holding the cards.)

The children with the cards stand in a row, with their backs to the king. (The children can be moved around between each go, to make this more challenging for older children.) The king must touch on the shoulder one of the children, who turns and shows their card. The king then does the same with another child, who also turns and shows their card. If the cards match, the king gets that debt repaid and the two children sit out. If the cards don't match, the children turn their backs again and the king tries to find another two matching cards, continuing until all the debts have been 'paid'.

A PICTURE YOU CAN'T SEE

The king was angry at first about the amount the official had borrowed, especially when he admitted that he couldn't pay it back. But then his expression turned to pity, and probably pleasure when he thought the man was grateful that he'd been so generous. But it didn't take long before he was angry again! Meanwhile, the other official was unhappily stuck in prison.

> *You will need a roll of plain lining paper, ordinary white kitchen candles, water-based paints made into a wash consistency, and large brushes.*

Let the children spread out along the length of the paper. Then, with a piece of candle each, they can choose to draw smiling, angry or sad faces, the king on his throne, the official 'behind bars', and so on. This will, of course, be quite hard to do, as they won't be able to see what they're drawing. When they've all finished, they can wash over the pictures with the water-based paints, and then their pictures will magically appear. But how difficult was this to do when they couldn't see, but had to rely on their sense of touch and imagination?

THE SENSE OF SMELL

THE SMELLY BILL

> *You will need a small handkerchief, sprayed with anything perfumed (a smelly bill from the king!).*

The children make a large circle, facing inwards. Choose one of the children to be the first official, and give him/her the bill. Of course, s/he will want to get rid of the bill, so s/he stands up and walks round the outside of the circle, dropping the bill behind the second official (any one of the others). S/he can pretend to drop the bill several times before s/he actually does so.

The others mustn't look—they have to use their noses! Once the bill has been dropped, the first official must try (without running!) to get back 'home' to their place without getting caught.

However, if the second official smells the bill behind them, s/he should grab it and chase after the first official (who now can start to run!), trying to get near enough to touch the first official's shoulder before s/he reaches 'home' and hand the smelly bill back. If the chaser is successful, the first official is out ('goes to jail'), but if the first official gets back to his/her place without getting caught, s/he can stay in the game and the second official must 'go to jail'.

Restart with a new first official.

GUESS WHAT?

The king has run out of money, so he has to put something else inside the moneybags.

You will need:
- *A large cardboard box, decorated to turn it into the king's treasure chest.*
- *At least the same number of large, uninflated balloons ('money bags') as there are children, into which (using a funnel) has been pushed some of the following: finely chopped apple, onion, cheese, celery, orange, lemon, herbs, curry powder, chocolate, sugar, coconut, ginger and so on. (NB: Use a different coloured balloon for each smell, and keep the openings pegged shut until needed for the activity.)*
- *Two sets of cards, with each of the smells used written on them.*

Divide the children into two teams. Place the treasure chest on a chair in front of, and equally between, the two teams. Beside each team should be a table, on which is laid out one set of the cards.

The first team member runs to the box, grabs an (unpegged) balloon, runs back with it to the rest of the team, who together decide on the smell from the options on the cards, and then place the balloon on that card.

Repeat until there are no balloons left in the treasure chest. Which team has more 'moneybags'? And which has more correct answers?

THE SENSE OF TASTE

THE TRUTH?

The king was fooled into thinking that the first official was really sorry about his huge debt. That was why he cancelled it. But that all changed when the king discovered the truth.

You will need:
- *A variety of bite-sized pieces of fruit, vegetables, cheese, fudge and so on.*
- *Larger pieces of strongly smelling and easily recognized items such as onion, chocolate, strong cheese, mint leaves, lemon and so on.*
- *Two blindfolds.*

Two children at a time can volunteer to sit on chairs and be blindfolded. Give each one a bite-sized item to taste, while at the same time holding a piece of onion, or something very different from what they're tasting, under their noses.

Can the children say what they are tasting? Or are they 'fooled' into thinking that the thing they can smell is what they're eating?

Then let them try the taste again without smelling anything different. Repeat as above, but also see how some of the children get on when holding their own noses, so that they can't smell anything at all. How does that affect the sense of taste?

WHO GETS THE GOLD?

The money that was loaned out by the king had come from taxes paid by the ordinary people, or from profit made by selling goods to surrounding countries. But the king would have considered it 'his' money. The first official behaved as though the money he'd borrowed from the king was his, and the second official had spent every penny of his loan.

> *You will need a large plastic or paper plate, and some foil-covered chocolate coins.*

The children sit in a circle, facing inwards. Working around the circle, whisper to each of them one of these names: First Official, Second Official, King. (This can be done in the same repeated order round the circle, or by giving almost all the children the same name, or randomly at will.)

Place the plate, with one chocolate coin on it, in the centre of the circle. Say that when the children hear their name, they can take the coin off the plate. Then say that the King, First Official or Second Official wants his money. Whoever has that name tries to get to the plate first to retrieve the chocolate coin—which could be several children or just one or two!

Replace the chocolate coin and either rename the children immediately, or wait till the next time round before doing so. Try to make sure all the children have a chance to claim one of the coins.

STEP INTO REFLECTION

To start the children thinking, a group of leaders could read this simple dramatization. A crown could be worn when the king's lines are spoken (Narrator 1) with two different hats for the first and second officials (Narrators 1 and 3) to help the children to follow the lines and make it more fun to watch.

Narrator 1: 'Give me my money back!'
Narrator 2: ...said the king.
Narrator 1: 'You've borrowed thousands of coins!'
Narrator 3: 'I haven't a penny!'
Narrator 2: ...the other man cried.
Narrator 1: 'Then it's to jail you're going,'
Narrator 2: ...the king replied.
Narrator 1: 'It's to jail you're going, right now!'
Narrator 3: 'I'm really so sorry!'
Narrator 2: ...the man cried out.
Narrator 3: 'Forgive me, that's all that I ask.'
Narrator 1: 'Oh, well, go on then, but don't do it again! And, by the way, you don't owe me a penny!'
Narrator 3: 'Yippee! Whoopeedoo!'
Narrator 2: ...the official yelled out.
Narrator 3: 'This clearly is my lucky day!'

Narrator 2: Then on the way out he gave a loud SHOUT! to a man whom he'd given a loan.
Narrator 3: 'Give me my money back!'
Narrator 2: ...he yelled.
Narrator 3: 'You've borrowed a hundred coins!'
Narrator 1: 'I haven't a penny,'
Narrator 2: ...the other man cried.
Narrator 3: 'Then it's to jail you're going,'
Narrator 2: ...the man replied.
Narrator 3: 'It's jail you're going, right now!'
Narrator 1: 'I'm really so sorry,'
Narrator 2: ...the man cried out.
Narrator 1: 'Forgive me, that's all that I ask.'
Narrator 3: 'Forgive you? Why should I?'

Well, why should he? What do the children think? Even when someone has been generous to us, is it really so easy to be generous, kind or thoughtful to someone else?

Are the richest people always the most generous? Or is the problem that they're sometimes less able to understand and be sympathetic towards people who lead lives so different from their own?

STEP INTO PRAYER

We may find other people's actions hard to forgive, but only when we ourselves become perfect will we be able to stop forgiving others!

Even Jesus, who was completely perfect, refused to condemn other people. He just said that when we realize we've done something wrong, we must as try as hard as we can never to do that thing again.

If one of our friends does something unkind to us, we'll probably forgive them, but we don't expect them to keep on being unkind! And the same thing goes for us.

This is a simple prayer about forgiving, with a familiar tune that everyone can dance to while they're saying it:

It's called 'Let's forgive again!' (to the tune of 'Let's Twist Again').

Let's forgive again, like we did last summer.
Let's forgive again, like we did last year.

Remember when Jesus told that story—
He said, 'Forgive again, just like I do to you.'

Oh, round and round forgiveness goes from me to you.
If I say sorry, and you say sorry, we're friends!

But down and down and worse and worse our world becomes,
if no one cares and no one shares a thing.

So let's forgive again, like we did last summer.
Let's forgive again, like we did last year.

Remember that everyone is different.
But Jesus loves
everyone the same.
Yeah!

Perhaps the children could make up a couple of other verses.
This would be a nice song to get the grown-ups to learn and dance along with.
Find out if someone knows the tune and how to dance the Twist!

STEP INTO THE STORY
OF ETERNITY

THE PARABLE OF THE GREAT FEAST

LUKE 14:15–24

OLD TESTAMENT LINK

When all is said and done, there might be some surprises around the table!

Jesus was doing a very rare thing for him—having dinner in the home of a Pharisee. It was the Sabbath and everyone else who'd been invited was watching Jesus closely, because they never knew what he was going to say or do next. Having him around was always exciting!

Now, Jesus had noticed how some of the other guests had each tried to take the best seats around the table—trying to give the impression that they were far more important than the rest (not realizing that Jesus was more important than all of them put together). But Jesus, of course, didn't complain. He simply started to tell a couple of little stories about how people should behave when invited to, or giving, a special meal.

Afterwards, one of the guests enthusiastically said, 'The greatest blessing of all is to be at the banquet in God's kingdom!'

They must have all agreed with that, but Jesus then told this story.

There was a rich man, he said, who decided to hold a great banquet in his home. He invited a lot of guests—it was a very big house!—and, when the food was finally all prepared, he sent out his servants to call on each guest to say that the party was ready. Would they please come?

However, amazingly—and very rudely!—one guest after another decided that he had something more important to do. The first one said, 'I've just bought some land and I must look it over. You'll have to excuse me.' Another said, 'I've just bought five teams of oxen, and I need to try them out, so I'm really too busy.' Still another said, 'Sorry, but I've just got married, so I certainly can't be there!' And so it went on.

When the servants reported back to their master that not one of his invited guests was going to arrive, the man was very, very angry. After all, he'd gone to a great deal of trouble and expense for them. So guess what he did? He said to his servants, 'Go as fast as you can to every street and alley in town. Bring in everyone who is poor or crippled, or blind or lame. They will be my guests.'

What a brilliant thing to do! However, even with all those people in the man's great house, there was still plenty of room for more people. So their master said, 'Go out along the back roads and lanes, and make people come in, so that my house will be full.' And then he added a final instruction to his servants: 'Not one of the guests I first invited will get even a bite of my food!'

Now, we're not told what the people listening to this parable thought about it, but they should have got the message that, at some time in all of our lives, God will give every single one of us an invitation to join him finally in heaven.

We can listen to him and accept the invitation, or we can spend our whole life being too busy doing other things, and miss the greatest party of all.

STEP INTO THE SENSES

THE SENSE OF SIGHT

YES OR NO?

God wants us always to say 'Yes' to him, no matter how busy we are. If the children were inviting their friends to a party, they'd hope everyone would say 'Yes' to them.

You will need:
- *Plain paper (at least 15 cm square), previously well creased to make sixteen smaller squares.*
- *One larger piece of paper, folded as above, to use as an example.*
- *Pens, pencils and scissors.*

YES	NO	YES	NO
NO	YES	NO	YES
YES	NO	YES	NO
NO	YES	NO	YES

Writing in the centre of each square, print YES / NO / YES / NO in the top four boxes, then NO / YES / NO / YES in the row below. Repeat for the next two rows (so that YES/ NO is always alternate both down and across).

Fold the paper along the creased lines to make a smaller folded square. This can be done in any way (left over right, right over left, forwards, backwards, top to bottom, side to side, or however you like).

Trim a couple of millimetres off each side of the smaller square, thus making sure all the folds are removed, and leaving you with sixteen separate squares of paper. Without altering which way up the squares are in your hand, lay them out in a line on the table.

Amazingly, either all eight 'Yes'es will be showing, or all eight 'No's! The children can now try this on each other. Whichever way the paper is folded, they will only ever finish up with either all 'Yes'es, or all 'No's.

WHO'S INVITED NOW?

The first invitations went to people who'd have been expected to dress up especially for the occasion, but the poor people who went in the end would have been wearing rags.

You will need:
- *Squares of card, about 6 x 6 cm, with a faint circle drawn in exactly the same position on one side of each card.*
- *Coloured pencils, felt tips or crayons.*
- *Sticks or straws plus sticky tape and glue.*

Each child will need two pieces of card, one stick or straw, and some crayons.

On one of the cards, using the faint circle for the face, they should draw the head and shoulders of someone with a smart hairstyle and tidy clothes. Taking the other card, and again using the circle as a guide, they should draw, say, a scruffy beard, an old hat, straggly hair, torn and dirty clothes and so on.

The straw should then be taped to the back of one of the cards so that one end sticks out below the card, some glue should be put on the back of the other card, and the cards stuck together (with both faces the same way up, and the straw in between them).

Holding the straw between their palms, and rolling it back and forth so that the card spins, the children can then see how the smart person changes into someone scruffy!

When everyone's hand is up, they each say who they think is standing behind them, then let them turn round to see if they were right.

Swap the two groups of children around and repeat the activity.

THE SENSE OF SOUND

CAN YOU HEAR ME?

God invites everyone to his amazing 'party', but not everyone hears the message.

> *You will need:*
> * *Chairs for half the number of children.*
> * *A couple of clean and empty yoghurt pots.*
> * *Two small plastic boxes, two sheets of A4 paper, two clean handkerchiefs.*

Sit half the children on the chairs, which should be well spread out in a line at one end of the room, facing the wall. Let these children take note of who the remaining children are (explaining that they'll be getting a nice invitation from one of them).

In order to disguise their voices, the remaining children can take a sheet of paper or handkerchief to speak against, or a box or yoghurt pot to speak into, or they can just alter the tone of their voice or put a hand over their mouth. Each of them should then go and stand behind one of the seated children and say, 'Come to the party!' in their disguised voice. The seated children should raise a hand when they think they know who is speaking.

KAZOO TIME!

How would those people who finally entered the rich man's house for the banquet have felt? It must have seemed as if it was their birthday, a million times over. They could hardly have helped feeling excited, and making a lot of noise. Wouldn't you?

> *You will need plenty of drinking straws (a variety of thicknesses and lengths), plus some scissors.*

The children can choose any length of straw, flattening one end so that a triangle can be cut off each side, thus creating a pointed end. The long straws can then have a small slot cut somewhere along their length for an added variety of sound. (Flatten the straw a little to help make the cut.)

Putting the pointed end to their lips and covering/releasing the slot, if there is one, they can make a variety of sounds with their home-made kazoos. They can choose a tune and all try to play it. Individuals could also think of a simple tune, play it, and see if anyone can guess what it is.

THE SENSE OF TOUCH

EYES ON THE ENDS OF THEIR FINGERS!

The blind people at the rich man's banquet would have had to use their sense of touch to persuade themselves that it was all real. Because of that, they would have experienced far more about their surroundings than those who simply looked.

> *You will need six to eight items of the following types:*
> - *Soft/silky/furry/lacy material.*
> - *Anything made from ivory, marble or stone.*
> - *Things made out of carved wood.*
> - *Jewellery or beads with different shapes and textures.*
> - *Plastic cup with a raised pattern.*
> - *Picture with a rough or patterned surface.*
> - *Metal box with pressed-out decorations.*
> - *A baby's toy.*

Lay the items out on a table. Ask the children to walk around the table and simply look at the items, then go and sit down with their backs to the table. How many can they remember? Choose a child to describe one, as fully as they can. Then let that same child go back to the table and, with their eyes closed, feel the item they've just described, then return to the other children.

Ask the child to describe the item again. How much more can they say about it, now that they've felt it and not just looked at it? Let all the children return to the table and, closing their eyes, feel each item. Sitting back down, it should now be much easier for them to remember every item on the table, and describe them quite fully.

NOT SO EASY?

> *You will need:*
> - *Pencils and paper.*
> - *Plastic beakers and water in water jugs.*
> - *Bread, butter and plastic knives.*
> - *Toothpaste and toothbrushes.*
> - *Items of clothing with plenty of fastenings.*
> - *Blindfolds for half the number of children.*

Lay out the above items on a table (duplicate, if necessary), then blindfold half the children, explaining that, using these items, their task will be to:
- write their name
- pour themselves a drink, without spilling any water
- spread the butter on the bread
- put toothpaste on a toothbrush
- do up all the fastenings

The others will enjoy watching them have difficulty in doing what are normally easy, everyday tasks—but will they do any better when it's their turn?

THE SENSE OF SMELL

WHICH SMELLS THE NICEST?

The food at the wealthy man's banquet would have been very elaborate, using herbs and ingredients from far distant countries. The wine would have been mixed with honey. There would have been

three main courses. The puddings would have been very rich, sweet pastries and the whole meal would have lasted for hours. It would have been nothing remotely like the food usually eaten by the poor people who went to the banquet in the end! Probably, at first, they even thought they wouldn't like the food, because it looked and smelt so different.

You will need:
- *A small dish of mashed potato; plus a duplicate with red food colouring mixed in.*
- *Small squares of crustless white bread; duplicate spotted with green and blue.*
- *Little pot containing butter; duplicate with the butter coloured purple.*
- *Small cubes of plain sponge cake; duplicate with plenty of blue dots.*
- *Ordinary water; duplicate with green food colouring.*
- *Large tray for each set of the above, plus spoons, butter knife, and beakers.*

First of all, bring out the tray with the oddly coloured food and drink, inviting all the children to smell everything on the tray, saying what each item smells like. They can then say what they think everything on the tray actually is. One or two should be invited to eat something off the tray—if there's anything they think will taste nice. If they eat anything, what did it taste like?

Now swap trays to the one containing the uncoloured food. Repeat the above.

Which food tray did they prefer? Which smelt the nicest? Older children will probably have guessed that the food and drink was, in fact, the same on each tray, but how easy was it to ignore the strange colours? And did the colours affect how they anticipated that the food would both smell and taste?

THE TASTE OF A SMELL

Even the smells inside the rich man's house would have seemed strange at first to the poor people. There would have been perfumes and flowers, rich materials on the walls and floors, as well as all the wonderful food. It might seem strange, but those smells would have affected how the food tasted!

You will need sandwiches, cut up into small squares, made with some or all of the following: peanut butter, various jams, cheese spread, mashed egg, Marmite, honey.

The children can volunteer to try eating any one of the above, while smelling another. Can they tell what they are actually smelling? How much is their sense of taste confusing their sense of smell?

THE SENSE OF TASTE

SHARING THE FEAST

The man wanted to share what he had, so everyone had something to enjoy. Learning to share is one of the hardest things in life, but also one of the most important.

You will need hoop-shaped crisps, small sweets, and straws.

Each child puts a hoop on each of their fingers. When that's done, they must immediately put their arms straight out in front of them. They mustn't bring their hands towards their face, so the problem is how they now manage to eat the hoops.

The answer is, of course, that they have to let someone else eat their hoops. But they also have to organize themselves so that it's fair on everyone! Put the sweets on small plates and give each child a straw, which they must use to pick up one of the sweets. (They'll have to figure out that they need to put the straw against the sweets, and suck!)

Having got that far, how do they manage to actually eat their sweet? (Taking someone else's hand, holding it flat, and letting the sweet drop from the end of their straw, would be one way.)

FOOD FOR THOUGHT!

The banquet tables would have been full of some wonderful food and drink. The children can make their own banquet, to celebrate the fact that God loves us right now, and always will.

Cheesy Grins: Spread cream cheese on crackers, then make a smiling face with raisins or sultanas.

Crunchy Crackers: Mix soft cheese and crunchy peanut butter together, then spread the mix on cream crackers.

Smartie Rolls: Cut any kind of Swiss roll into thin slices, lay them out on a plate, then push Smarties into the jam filling.

Peanut Scrunchies: Cut finger rolls in half through the middle, spread with a mixture of smooth peanut butter and soft cheese, then top with crushed crisps.

Hot Choc Special: Make hot chocolate drinks, then float a marshmallow on the top.

Milk Shake Special: Use any flavour of 'whip' mix, double the quantity of milk shown on the packet, and whisk well. Serve with straws.

Creamy Whip: Whisk vanilla ice-cream and yoghurt (without bits of fruit) together, then add whipped cream. Pour into a glass and top with spray cream. Serve with a spoon.

STEP INTO REFLECTION

Close your eyes and imagine you're huddled up in the doorway of an empty shop.

It's evening and beginning to rain. The ground is hard and cold beneath you, so you can't even sit comfortably, let alone sleep very well. You have nothing with you except for the torn, old clothes you're wearing. You're very, very hungry—it's been three days since your last meal, and that was just some dry bread that a passing stranger threw at you. Your stomach aches with hunger and you feel so tired.

How do you feel?

You have no home and no work. And it's been like this for so many years that you can't remember living in any other way.

How do you feel?

Suddenly, someone's at your side. They're shaking you. You wish they'd leave you alone! Do they want you to move? You're not doing any harm where you are. You don't want to have to go searching for somewhere else to go out of the rain. This doorway has been 'home' for several weeks now. You don't want to have to move.

But what's that they're saying? You're invited to a what? A banquet? Now you know you must be dreaming! But they're shaking you harder now, telling you that you must get up and go with them. There's a very rich man who wants you—*you!*—to share his great feast in what sounds like a palace. And he won't take No for an answer!

How do you feel?

You can hardly believe it, but you're now walking through the grand gates of a fabulous house—and not just you, either. You're surrounded by the familiar faces of others who've been sleeping on the streets, like you. Some are just penniless, like you. Others are blind or lame, deaf or disabled. And you've all been invited to this great feast!

How do you feel?

As you walk into the most enormous room

you've ever seen, filled with the most enormous table, covered with the most mouth-watering food, you wonder if you've died and gone to heaven! Surely this can't be real? Someone at your side says, 'All the rich people in town should have been here at this banquet, but they were too busy to come. That's why we're here.'

How do you feel?

The wonderful meal is over. You've eaten as much as you possibly can and have a bag full of food to take away with you. And it's time to go— back to the street, back to your doorway.

How do you feel?

Many years later, it's the end of your life and now you're looking at another, even more fantastic banquet, an even bigger and more wonderful party. It's God's party—for you. And this time it goes on for ever and ever.

How do you feel?

STEP INTO PRAYER

God speaks to us in a million different ways throughout our lives. There isn't a single moment when he isn't listening for us to speak to him. And we can do that in a million different ways, too! He'll always hear us. But do we always hear *him*? This prayer is called 'Ask me again!'

Sorry, God, were you talking?
Didn't catch what you said.
Could you repeat it? I'll listen—
if there's room in my head!
'Cos you must understand
there's a lot going on—
and I don't want to miss any of it.

I'm wondering, you see,
if there's pizza for tea.
(Hey, does anyone know what's on telly?)
This computer game is just brill,
don't you know—I've reached the last
level. Can you wait half a mo?
And talk to me after. I'll listen! I will!
And I promise I won't miss any of it.

But there's lots going on,
and I don't have much time.
Got to practise my football... karate...
Gymnastics and dance... piano...
no chance I'd want to miss any of it.

I've friends coming round, we've got so
much to say, and games we must play,
and jokes we must tell,
And places to go and things we must see—
and we just cannot miss any of it.

So, sorry God, were you talking?
Didn't catch what you said.
If you repeat it, I'll listen
(I'll make room in my head!)
And though there's lots going on
(you do understand),
I'll try not to miss any of it.

It would be good to finish with a song! This can be sung to the tune of 'O when the saints go marching in'. The children can march around the room and play instruments such as tambourines and cymbals, or anything that appears in this book, such as the kazoos, the shakers and the cardboard box drums, to add to the fun!

O when the guests go marching in,
O when the guests go marching in.
I want to be at that banquet!
When the guests go marching in.

When Jesus sits among the guests,
When Jesus sits among the guests,
I want to be at that banquet!
When Jesus sits among the guests.

O when they give a great big cheer,
O when they give a great big cheer,
I'm going to shout as loud as I can!
When they give a great big cheer.

Repeat first verse.

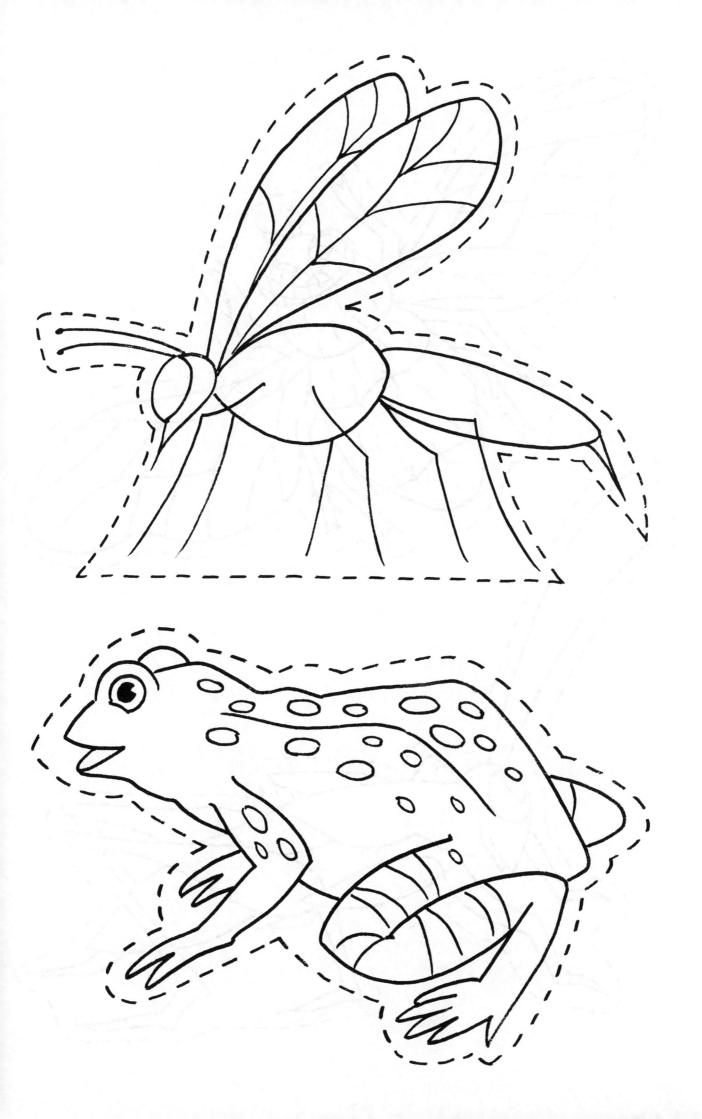

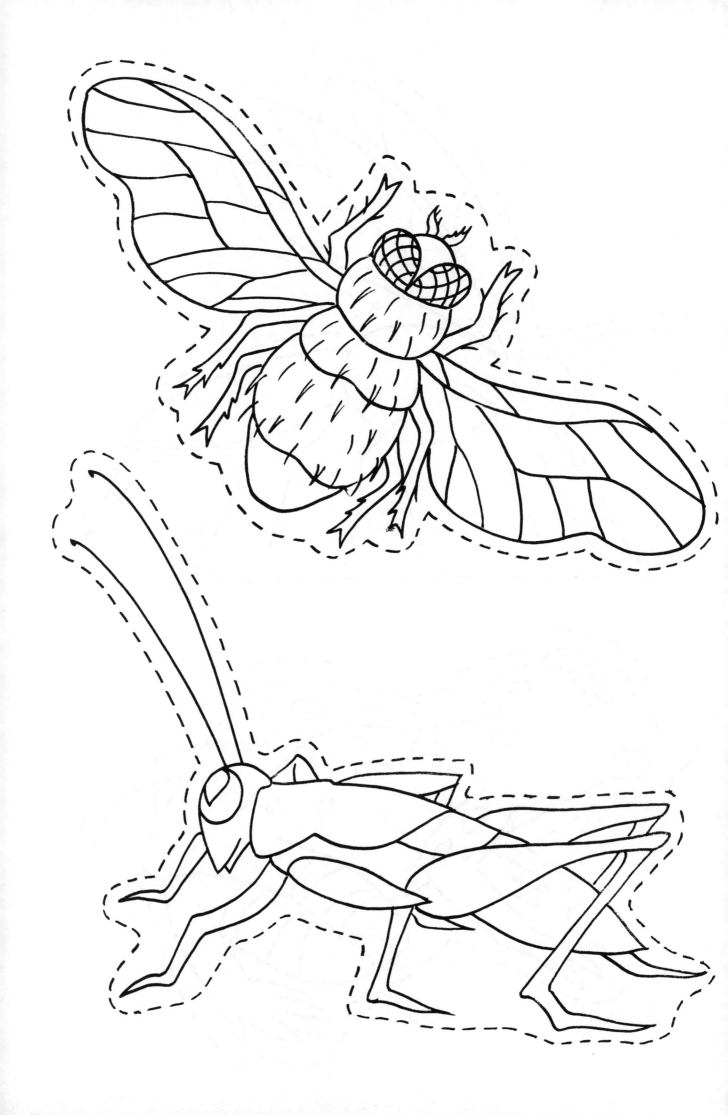

✶ ✶ ✶ ✶ ✶ ✶ ✶

OTHER RESOURCES
FROM BARNABAS

REF 1 84101 224 6, £8.99

This book provides 40 five-minute read-aloud stories of people who have lived their lives for God. Each story links to a key Bible passage, includes its own prayer, has suggested activities including crafts, drama and creative writing, and shows a symbol for the saint and suggestions for songs. In the centre of the book there is a photocopiable chart where all the saints' symbols are given. The saints fall into four categories: Bible saints from the New Testament, such as St Paul; historical and legendary saints, such as St George; worldwide saints, such as St Francis of Assisi; and contemporary saints, such as Mother Teresa.

★ ★ ★ ★ ★ ★ ★

OTHER RESOURCES FROM BARNABAS

Ref 1 84101 223 8, £12.99

Teachers cover the major festivals every year and new approaches are welcome both for them and for the pupils. The book comprises twelve units, each using a variety of stimuli to introduce the festivals of Harvest, Christmas, Easter, New Year, Pentecost and Mothering Sunday. This material is designed to contribute to the bank of suitable and relevant resources for these times, providing an innovative way into Christian festivals and encouraging pupil participation at Key Stage One.

Visit the brf website www.brf.org.uk

★ ★ ★ ★ ★ ★ ★

OTHER RESOURCES FROM BARNABAS

REF 1 84101 243 2, £12.99

Ideal for busy teachers and church leaders who have endless demands on their time and energy and need stories that jump off the page, into the imagination and, from there, into daily life.

Drawn from all four Gospels, the pieces are 'unplugged' in that they get to the heart of the biblical text, reflecting the life of Jesus in action: who he is, what he said and what he did. Some tell the story, some explore an aspect of the original account. Many pieces include children. Some pieces are meant to be performed, some to be enjoyed quietly; but the overall aim is to have fun and enjoy unplugging the Gospels!

Visit the brf website www.brf.org.uk